BAD THERAPY

BAD THERAPY
Master Therapists
Share Their Worst Failures

Jeffrey A. Kottler, Ph.D.
and Jon Carlson, Psy.D, Ed.D.

Brunner-Routledge
New York and Hove

Published in 2003 by
Brunner-Routledge
29 West 35th Street
New York, NY 10001
www.brunner-routledge.com

Published in Great Britain by
Brunner-Routledge
27 Church Rd.
Hove, East Sussex
BN3 2FA
www.brunner-routledge.co.uk

10 9 8 7 6 5 4 3 2

Library of Congress Cataloging-in-Publication Data
Kottler, Jeffrey A.
  Bad therapy : master therapists share their worst failures / Jeffrey A. Kottler and
Jon Carlson
      p. cm.
  Includes bibliographical references.
    ISBN 0–415–93322–6 (alk. paper) 0–415–93323–4 (pbk.)
  1. Psychiatric errors. I. Carlson, Jon. II. Title.
    RC455.3 .E76 K68 2002
    616.89—dc21
                                                      2002008676

CONTENTS

ABOUT THE AUTHORS

JEFFREY A. KOTTLER, Ph.D. is Chair of the Counseling Department at California State University, Fullerton. He has authored over 45 books for practitioners (*On Being a Therapist, The Imperfect Therapist, Compassionate Therapy, Making Changes Last*); students (*Nuts and Bolts of Helping, Introduction to Therapeutic Counseling, Learning Group Leadership, Theories in Counseling and Therapy*); teachers (*On Being a Teacher, Succeeding With Difficult Students*); and the public (*Private Moments, Secret Selves, Travel That Can Change Your Life, The Language of Tears, The Last Victim*).

Jeffrey has been an educator for 25 years. He has worked as a teacher, counselor, and therapist in preschool, middle school, mental health centers, crisis centers, universities, community colleges, and private practice. He has served as a Fulbright Scholar and Senior Lecturer in Peru (1980) and Iceland (2000), as well as worked in dozens of countries as a consultant and trainer specializing in multicultural issues.

JON CARLSON, Psy.D., Ed.D. is Distinguished Professor of Psychology and Counseling at Governors State University, University Park, Illinois and a Psychologist with the Wellness Clinic in Lake Geneva, Wisconsin. Jon is the author of 25 books, 100 journal articles, serves as Editor of *The Family Journal*, and is the developer of over 100 videotapes. These instructional videos feature today's leading experts in the fields of psychotherapy, family therapy, brief therapy, substance abuse and treatment, parenting, and couples education. Dr. Carlson has received Distinguished Services awards from the American Psychological Association, the American Counseling Association, International Association of Marriage and Family Counselors, and the North American Society of Adlerian Psychology.

A few of Jon's best known books include: *Brief Therapy With Individuals and Couples, The Disordered Couple, Interventions and Strategies in Counseling and Psychotherapy*, and *Family Counseling: Strategies and Issues*.

PREFACE

This is a book that reveals, with surprising honesty, the worst mistakes of the best therapists. Told through the narratives of their most stunning failures, two dozen of the world's most famous practitioners talk about their mistakes, misjudgments, and miscalculations that haunt them to this day. From such stories, readers are offered a rare glimpse into the hearts and minds of the profession's most famous authors, theoreticians, and leaders.

WHEN THINGS GO WRONG

Therapists have a long history of inventing ways to disown our misjudgments and mistakes. We blame our clients for not trying hard enough or being unmotivated. We ascribe negative outcomes to circumstances beyond our control—meddling family members, organic or environmental factors, time constraints. We call our clients ugly names like *borderline* or *obstructive* or *resistant*. All this means is that the people we are trying so hard to help are not cooperating with our best efforts, or more likely, they aren't meeting our expectations.

In moments of honesty, or when our guards are down, all of us are haunted by those we couldn't help. We are especially bothered by those (we hope) few occasions when the bad therapy occurred as a result of our own blunders. We pushed too hard too fast; we misread the situation; we missed crucial information. Our own personal issues were triggered. We were less than tactful. We bungled the diagnosis. We were less than skillful in executing an intervention. In these ways, and a hundred others, we flat out blew the interview. We chased the client away. We may have set treatment back significantly. Then, if we could get away with it, we pretended it all never happened. Denial and defensiveness provide a convenient means to bury our mistakes, sometimes to help us pretend they never happened in the first place.

Progress notes become less than accurate, reports to supervisors less than fully disclosing. The name of the game is "cover your butt," protect yourself from malpractice claims and censures from supervisors. And many of us collude to blame the client whenever possible. When that doesn't work, then it must be some other third party who is ruining our perfectly good efforts.

There is no doubt that the subject of this book is very threatening and challenging to talk about in frank and honest ways. Who wants to discuss the worst disappointments and disasters they have faced? Who wants to read a book about the worst stuff in our profession?

If we are going to cover this subject, then we decided to do so with a more upbeat emphasis by focusing not just on what went wrong but also on what can be learned from the mistakes. Growth and learning, after all, often result from making sense of things that go wrong. This is especially the case when we are reflective and systematic about deconstructing the sequence of events and making sense of the experience. This is no less than what we expect of our clients.

THE PARTICIPANTS

The major premise of this project was that if we could get the most prominent practitioners and thinkers in the field to talk about their worst work, then perhaps this would create a forum for others to discuss their lapses, mistakes, misjudgments, and failures more openly and constructively.

We selected our subjects based on what we believe to be their impact and influence on the profession. They had to be "prominent," which we defined as: (1) having a body of published work that is known to many practitioners; (2) having clinical experience spanning over many years to draw on; (3) a willingness to participate. We leaned heavily on personal contacts, especially those from Jon Carlson's film series, *Psychotherapy with the Experts*. We tried for a cross-section of representative styles and theoretical orientations.

The reader may wonder why certain people were included and others were not part of this investigation. As you might expect, some people respectfully declined—for very good reasons. Why, after all, would people who have achieved prominence risk their reputations by talking in public about the worst example of his or her work? Why indeed?

Every one of the contributors to this book volunteered to participate primarily because they had already worked with one of us in some capacity. There was a preexisting relationship built on some degree of trust and mutual respect. They felt reassured perhaps that we would not use what they shared with us to hurt them or take advantage of them in some way. Many of these prominent people had been burned before by others who took advantage of them.

We were not surprised that about a third of the people we contacted declined the invitation; rather we were amazed at the two thirds who agreed to participate so enthusiastically. We told them that this would be fun, but they knew far better that even if our conversations with them were interesting, they were bound to bring up a lot of painful stuff.

THE METHODOLOGY

After scheduling phone interviews weeks in advance, we reserved an hour for the two of us to interview each contributor. We sent each of them a list of questions we would be asking them so they had time to think about them ahead of time. In some cases, this structure was abandoned when the conversation drifted to other interesting areas.
The questions included:

1. What were you thinking about as you anticipated and reflected on this conversation?
2. What is bad therapy to you?
3. When you think of the worst therapy session you ever did, what immediately comes to mind? Describe what happened in detail.
4. What made this session so awful for you (and/or your client)?
5. What is it like for you to revisit this experience now, and talk about it publicly?
6. What are some things that you did, or did not do, that you regret or would have done differently?
7. What did you learn from this experience?
8. What could others learn from this episode and how you've processed it?
9. How do you think that others could profit from speaking more frankly and honestly about their worst efforts?

Each of the interviews was recorded, then transcribed. We then wrote up the discussion in more readable prose, using both dialogue and narrative description. We were able to preserve both the accuracy and tone of each conversation, but also to present it in a way that makes for riveting reading.

Each chapter was sent to each participant so that he or she could check it for accuracy. The vast majority of the participants were quite pleased with how things turned out, but also a bit apprehensive about appearing so vulnerable.

ACKNOWLEDGMENTS

Our third partner in the process of organizing the manuscript was Laurie Johnson, who transcribed the tapes in a way that made our jobs so much easier. We also wish to acknowledge the contributions of Diane Blau, who collaborated with Jeffrey Kottler on an earlier book published many years ago about therapy failures. We also wish to thank Tim Julet, formerly of Brunner-Routledge, who first signed this book, and Emily Epstein for shepherding it through the editorial process. We wish to applaud the courage and the openness of the contributors to this project. We hope that you feel as proud of your efforts as we do.

We are also grateful for the constructive feedback from our reviewers who made some helpful suggestions for revising the manuscript. Thanks to Howard Rosenthal, Keven Fall, Samuel T. Gladding, and Robert E. Wubbolding.

Introduction

THE GOOD, THE BAD, AND THE UGLY
Parameters of Bad Therapy

We were sitting around kidding one another about how funny and interesting it would be if only the leaders in our field would be more frank and open about their mistakes. After all, our own therapy looks nothing like those "perfect" demonstrations you see on videos by the experts. And we should know: Jeffrey has been studying failure for over 30 years and Jon has produced over 100 videos by the greatest therapists of the past century (*Psychotherapy with the Experts*), watching not only the sessions that made the final cut, but also the ones that were erased.

We remember the earliest years of our own training in which we were exposed to the famous "Gloria" tape wherein the three most prominent practitioners of their day—Fritz Perls, Albert Ellis, and Carl Rogers—all worked with the same client. However bizarrely divergent their approaches, they all looked pretty effective to us. It wasn't so much what they did that was impressive—it was their poise and confidence.

Rather than having the desired effect of bolstering our commitment to the field and improving our conceptual mastery, we left the class despondent and discouraged. How could we ever become good enough in this new profession to help people with anything near the degree of mastery of these experts? They were calm and self-assured, ready to face anything the client might present. They had all the answers (even if they were all different).

Over the next three decades, we continued to watch other therapy videos and live demonstrations as a way to improve our clinical skills and understanding of this complex business we call therapy. We have gotten so much better over the years with practice. Supervision has helped a lot, so has consultation with trusted colleagues, attending workshops,

1

getting more education, reading books, and writing in a journal. Probably more than anything else, being a client in therapy has taught us about what works best. Yet in spite of all the advanced degrees we've attained, the books we've read (and written), we've come to the conclusion that practicing therapy is absolutely the most challenging and fun professional endeavor because we will never get it right—not even close. There is too much to learn in a hundred lifetimes, too much new information to digest, new studies to review, new approaches to master, new interventions to practice. To our clients, students, readers, and supervisees, we might look as though we know what we're doing (and we are pretty good at helping people most of the time), but believe us when we tell you that we are nowhere close to where we would like to be.

SELECTING THE BEST PERFORMANCE

When Jon asked Jeffrey to do a demonstration video for his series on *Psychotherapy with the Experts,* he was certainly honored and flattered. Then, he thought to himself: "But wait, I'm still an unfinished product. However I used to do therapy in my 20s, 30s, or 40s, or even last year, is not how I operate any longer."

Given the pressure Jeffrey puts on himself to do better, he was surprised he felt so little apprehension at the prospect of performing on stage with the cameras going. As the producer of this series, Jon was a master of putting these things together. He had built a professional studio and during the 1990s had worked with 50 of the greatest therapists, filming their work for posterity. He was thus highly skilled not only at producing excellent film products but also putting his subjects at ease.

Jon wanted Jeffrey to see three different clients so as to make sure we had a "good" example of his work. Jeffrey protested, suggesting that one was plenty—however the session turned out would be a fair representation of the way he works. "Besides," he explained, "I'm sick of seeing so-called experts strut their best stuff." He pointed out that some of his most productive sessions were hideously awkward and ugly. They rarely looked as smooth, polished, and controlled as what he'd seen on the TV screen.

Jon agreed but said, "Humor me. Do three of them so we have some choices." Jon has learned over the years when to take Jeffrey seriously and when to change the subject. This time he preferred to pretend he was kidding.

They agreed on a plan and did tape three consecutive sessions with different clients. One was pretty darn good. Within the span of 45 minutes Jeffrey managed to throw in no less than 17 different interventions to highlight his so-called theory of client-focused integrative therapy, the name that Jon used for his work since at the time Jeffrey didn't have one. The client was cooperative, eager, and they hit it off beautifully. After the interview was over Jeffrey was genuinely sorry that they wouldn't have the chance to work together in the future.

If the first session was good, the second was pretty mediocre. The client rambled and chattered, Jeffrey listened attentively and compassionately. Normally, it would have been quite acceptable for an initial interview—unless you were asked to show your best stuff in front of a live audience, three camera operators, assorted film crew, and a future audience composed of the next generation of therapists. The session was boring and superficial—not much happened.

If the first one was good, the second one bad, then you probably guessed the third was ugly. The guy only came in because he was pressured by his girlfriend (the previous client). He wouldn't talk. He wouldn't follow Jeffrey's lead, wouldn't respond to his increasingly desperate attempts to get him to move in any direction. Actually, he was like so many of the clients we've seen over the years—reluctant, terrified, and unwilling to go very deep until we got to know one another better.

After what felt like several hours, the director flashed a sign indicating there were still 30 minutes left in the session. Could they really have been together for only 15 minutes? Jeffrey felt the beginnings of a panic attack, wondering what the hell he could possibly do with the interminable time they had left—all with the cameras running and the audience scrutinizing his every move.

Feeling he had little to lose, Jeffrey took a deep breath, squinted into the blinding lights, and held out his hand to stop the young man from continuing to report on why he didn't trust anyone outside his family, and never would.

"Look," Jeffrey told him in a conspiratorial voice, "you don't really want to be doing this right now." He waited a beat or two, then added: "And neither do I." The client sat back in his chair and regarded Jeffrey with suspicion. He thought he was home-free, easily able to outlast the therapist through the next half hour without saying or revealing much.

"Why don't you give me a break?" Jeffrey pressed him, then felt ashamed he was putting the focus on his own needs. The client wasn't sure if Jeffrey was serious in changing the rules in midstream so he said nothing at all.

"Look," Jeffrey continued in a whisper, looking over his shoulder as if this part of the conversation would be private, "I'm dying out here. We've got three cameras going and all these people watching, and. . . . "

Before Jeffrey could go on any further, the client quickly jumped in to mollify him. He threw out a few bones, just what you'd expect under these ridiculous and artificial circumstances. Neither Jeffrey nor Jon was surprised by how miserably the session was proceeding. The real miracle was that the first client managed to do such a nice piece of work in such a public forum.

We wish we could say that Jeffrey's various interventions—first self-disclosure, then immediacy and confrontation—were a turning point that rescued what was otherwise a pretty ugly session. Instead, the session limped along, Jeffrey testing, probing, pushing, pulling, getting through the ordeal. It was actually a fairly typical first interview. The problem was that the world was watching and this was supposed to be a demonstration of perfection. After all, isn't that what people pay for when they buy such videos?

After it was all over, when we reviewed the three tapes, we realized how great a demonstration this last session really was. It didn't show what an expert Jeffrey was, nor did it fairly illustrate his theory of helping. What the session *did* highlight was how many ways he could have done better. The more Jeffrey thought about it, the more convinced he became that *this* was the one he wanted to use in the video.

Jeffrey said, "If the purpose of these videos is to teach people how to do better therapy, why show a near-perfect sample that will only make beginners feel inadequate by comparison? Show them this one and they'll have some hope. They'll say to themselves, 'Heck, even *I* can do better than that.'"

"You may be right," Jon agreed, but then reminded him that the purpose of the series was to demonstrate theories in action, not improve therapist morale. He had a point. When we later showed the video to students they laughed delightedly at Jeffrey's feeble and ineffective efforts to work with the guy. We realized that this session was what doing therapy is *really* like when nobody else is watching. It is often ugly and awkward, a struggle for both participants. And the way to get better at this craft is not just by watching experts who work fluidly, seamlessly, and effortlessly. There is also so much to learn from exploring our doubts and uncertainties.

FROM A VIDEO TO A BOOK

As in other disciplines, it is common for therapists to attend professional meetings, conferences, and workshops in which the best among us demonstrate their masterful skills. We watch videos, see life demonstrations, and read about their exploits in books. The masters display on stage their dazzling artistry and flawless execution of strategy, often "curing" their clients in a single encounter. They talk about seeming hopeless cases in which they uttered some magic incantation that produced a miraculous result. Likewise, the books that are so often published present cases and examples that are designed to support the theory and fortify the author's stature. It is all too rare for prominent practitioners to admit publicly that they feel lost, bungled cases, or otherwise failed themselves and their clients. The result is that the mere mortals among us compare ourselves to our mentors and consistently find ourselves wanting.

Attend any conference and you will see otherwise poised, confident, experienced therapists turn into groupies when in the presence of the "immortal ones." The masters are put on pedestals, badgered for autographs, and treated as the celebrities that they have become. When the therapists return to their own practices, their worst fears are confirmed when they find that the same methods they saw so (apparently) effortlessly modeled on stage don't work nearly as well with their own clients. There are many good reasons for this—lack of practice and limited confidence with a new strategy, to mention a few—but the real reason is that famous therapists rarely speak about their bad therapy. This makes it extremely difficult for others who must live with their own inadequacies.

It is in the spirit of debunking myths and speaking more frankly about what doing therapy is *really* like that we are pleased and honored to present to you the worst sessions of the best therapists. It is our hope that such courageous and honest revelations will make it easier for others to discuss more honestly their own limitations and weaknesses. It is only by confronting our own imperfections that we are able to truly learn and grow. And if this works for our clients, then it must work for us as well.

WHAT IS BAD THERAPY?

It's not easy to define bad therapy. As with everything else in life, it is all in the eye of the beholder. It is a subjective assessment of one or both participants in which relative meaning and value are ascribed to the outcome (Kottler & Blau, 1989). It is a judgment about satisfaction levels of performance. It is also conceived as the kind of blunders that take place when personal issues and countertransference processes interfere with sound judgment (Robertiello & Schoenewolf, 1987). Regardless of the particular definition, failure and poor performance are part of being human, and processing these experiences constructively is what leads to mastery of a profession (Conyne, 1999).

What is bad therapy to some may be desired outcomes to others. One therapist considers his worst work to have occurred when a client stormed out of his office because he wasn't responding to her stated needs.

His supervisor, however, considered it a masterful session in that he didn't collude with her self-defeating, hidden agenda. The therapist judges the quality of his work based on the assessment of his satisfied customer, whereas his supervisor looks at other criteria that are based on her informed, expert evaluation. About the only clear indication of failure is "when both parties agree there has been no apparent change" (Kottler & Blau, 1989, p. 13). We have to keep in mind, of course, that sometimes clients only pretend to change when they actually remain as stuck as ever; at other times, they act as though they are unhappy with the result when, in fact, they have made astounding progress. It is always a bit disorienting when we hear from clients' significant others who give reports very different from what we might observe or what the client says is going on (Kottler, 2001). And then there are the cases in which therapy appears to be worthless in the short-run but actually results in long-term benefits (Keith & Whitaker, 1985). Bugental (1988) adds even more complexity to the challenge of defining what constitutes bad therapy by mentioning that *every* session includes features that are both good and bad.

Surely just as there is a consensus on "best practices" there must also be rough agreement on what is lousy treatment. If the client ends up worse than before therapy started, and continues to deteriorate after the sessions end prematurely, that would definitely be poor work. Likewise if the client appears to improve significantly we might conclude that the therapy was a success. The glitch in this reasoning, of course, is what "appears" to be occurring may not, in fact, be what is really happening. What happens when the positive effects don't persist very long and the behavior returns to baseline levels? Or what if the effects simply have a delayed reaction? Can we ever really know what impact we have on clients when we consider the accumulative influence that takes place over time? Perhaps our efforts were helpful or harmful after all, but the results don't show up until months or years later.

In a qualitative study of what leads to impasses in therapy, Hill, Nutt-Williams, Heaton, Thompson, and Rhodes (1996) interviewed 12 experienced therapists who were working with relatively severe cases in long-term treatment. They found that the variables that were most associated with these impasses included client characteristics (severity of pathology, history of interpersonal conflict), therapist characteristics (therapist mistakes, countertransference), and problems related to the therapeutic contract in which there was a lack of consensus about treatment goals. In a review of empirical studies distinguishing between good and bad therapy, Stiles, Gordon, and Lani (2002) found that two aspects of the sessions were most significant: the depth or power of the therapy, and how smoothly things proceed. They point out, however, that often clients and therapists don't agree about how smoothly or deeply the work is proceeding. These differences may be the result of different expectations for treatment.

We have all experienced the phenomenon in which we think we have done our absolutely best work and the client hardly notices at all, or offers the opinion that what we did was a waste of time. There are other times when we have blundered badly, or been functioning on autopilot, barely paying attention to what is going on, yet the client found the work to be downright miraculous.

When clients are asked what they consider to be bad therapy, they often mention what Estrada and Holmes (1999) found in their study of couple's assessments of marital therapy. Most clients cited that they found the experience lousy when the therapists were passive, when they wasted time, when they were unclear about their expectations, when they weren't empathic and understanding, and when they didn't keep things safe. Perhaps not surprisingly, clients find therapy to be less than helpful when therapists don't do what they want and expect; likewise, therapists judge the treatment as bad when clients are not cooperative. Clearly we are dealing with a complex, interactive phenomenon in which poor outcomes result from contributions by the therapist, the client, the situation, and external forces.

LEARNING FROM OUR WORST WORK

Commenting on a series of narratives written by therapists about a case of failure, Hollon (1995) suggests that the best person we might consult about the impasses is not only our supervisor, but also our client. It doesn't matter if the client's feedback is accurate or not, Hollon contends, since it represents the one perception that most powerfully influences the result.

The bottom line is what can be learned from our failures and miscues. As entertaining as these stories from our profession's most masterful practitioners might be, the key question to ask ourselves is what we can learn from their mistakes, and what we can learn from our own.

Chapter 1

JEFFREY A. KOTTLER
The Thing Is

When I first greeted Frances in the waiting room, I couldn't help but notice that she was already in the middle of a conversation: However, she was alone. " . . . granddaughter isn't usually that bad. I think her mother knows this. I've told her so many times. . . . "

"Hi Frances," I said, far more cheerfully than I felt.

She glanced up for a second, then brushed by me as she walked into my office and planted herself in a chair. She continued the conversation with me even though I was beyond her view, still standing at the door.

Frances was a big woman who walked very, very slowly. She was probably in her mid-70s although her dyed brown hair and carefully applied makeup made her look ageless to me—like the prototypical grandmother. I'd rather not confess this so early, but there is no doubt that she reminded me of the worse characteristics of my own grandmother; she was controlling, meddling, and an expert at instilling guilt. To this day, I am still occasionally startled into shame because I haven't called my grandmother lately—she died over 10 years ago.

"It's not like I haven't warned her," Frances continued, actually looking at me for the first time. I couldn't remember who she was supposed to be warning, but I knew it was hopeless to ask for clarification. She usually just ignored me.

I sighed, but mostly to myself. This was how our conversations usually started. Frances was so desperate for someone to listen to her that as soon as she heard my footsteps approaching the door, she'd launch into her litany of complaints. I guess she figured we could cover more ground that way. She wanted to suck every second of my attention she could.

In some ways, this was the easiest case I had ever handled. There were no debilitating symptoms I had to address, no emergency situation or crisis that had to be resolved. So far as I knew, Frances hadn't yet declared a goal that she wanted to work toward. It seemed that all she wanted to do was talk, and have someone, anyone, even someone she paid, to listen to her. It seemed like a simple enough assignment.

However, I became a therapist in the first place because I like to talk. At the very least, I enjoy some friendly, or even spirited, dialogue. After having spent a half-dozen sessions together, it quickly became apparent this old lady was not going to let me get a single word in. Believe me: I tried.

Well, I noticed that I'm doing *it* again, the *it* being that I'm blaming Frances for being an uncooperative, difficult client instead of recognizing that I was being a lousy therapist. In my own defense, let me say that even by my own exacting standards, I am actually quite a skilled practitioner. I even help people most of the time, and it doesn't take that long. But true confession time: this was just about the worst session I ever did, and I've had my share of doozies.

Let's see. There was the time I got so mad at a young woman who wouldn't dump her abusive boyfriend that I fired her in a moment of frustration, told her not to come back because I couldn't help her. She looked at me with complete despair and then left without a word. When I later called to apologize, she refused to speak with me ever again. I hope she got better care elsewhere.

Then there was the woman who decided to control our first interview by challenging my qualifications. Rather than going with the flow, I decided to fight back. I was feeling threatened but didn't realize it at the time. Within the first 15 minutes, I surrendered, telling her I didn't think we were a good match and that she should find someone else, someone "better qualified." Okay, so I tend to pout a little.

Once I told her to leave, she refused to do so, claiming that I was the only one who could help her (if I'd had a supervisor on this case, I would have told him or her that this was a brilliantly executed paradoxical directive). It took another hour to pry her out of the chair. She was so angry with me she spent the next 3 days leaving threatening messages on my answering machine, talking until she filled up the tape. Then she started sending me presents ordered from the shopping channel, accompanied by cryptic notes that announced that maybe the enclosed item would help me to recover from my problems. I was certainly curious to see what was inside, but not enough to open them. Could have been a bomb.

It's nice to reminisce, I know, but back to Frances. What made *this* session so memorably awful is that there was really very little I had to do to help her: just listen compassionately; show her some respect and empathy; make her feel cared for.

Because she wasn't meeting my expectations as a good client—she was neither interesting, entertaining, or even in obvious pain—I didn't feel she was deserving of my full attention. I don't need *that* much from my clients, but I like them to change, to do it quickly, and then to be grateful (but not *too* grateful). Frances, however, was boring and she rambled a lot. She'd go off on a rant as if I wasn't even in the room. When I'd interrupt her with some brilliant interpretation, she'd ignore me. This really hurt my feelings, not to mention my sense of competence. So I'd pout.

During this one particularly bad session, Frances had been going on for some time about how her daughter was such an inadequate mother because she wouldn't handle things exactly the same way that Frances would. I must say that I was not only feeling spectacularly bored, but also angry. It was as if she were my own father scolding me because I wasn't bringing up my son right.

For a variety of reasons, I decided I'd had quite enough of this stuff. I hadn't been listening to her anyway for the previous several minutes, having enjoyed an elaborate fantasy about where I wanted to visit for my next trip. What the heck—she wouldn't let me talk anyway so I might as well leave the room in my head. At one point, I even pictured myself tiptoeing out of the door and returning about the time our session was over. She'd probably never notice I was gone, I complained to myself.

Finally, I'd had enough. I had to *do* something. It seemed ridiculous that I was being paid to just sit there. Didn't she know how smart and insightful I was? Couldn't she realize how much I could help her, if only she'd let me say something?

"Frances," I interrupted her in voice that was hoarse from underuse. " . . . got an A– on his paper but this mother never said. . . . "

"Frances," I tried again, this time loud enough to startle her. This saintly grandmother looked at me with a wounded expression and I started to feel terribly guilty, not because I had so rudely interrupted but because I had long ago stopped listening to her altogether. This gave me a brilliant idea.

"Look," I said in a more moderate tone, "I need to say a few things to you. Can you listen for a minute?"

She crossed her arms and waited, but I could tell she was irritated with me. I noticed her glance at the clock as if to remind me that whatever I had to say, it had better be quick because she had a lot more ground to cover. I had been dying for this opportunity and now that it was finally here, I was feeling hesitant, thinking maybe I should just slip back into my accustomed role. "Look," I said, starting again, "you have so much to say. You *always* have so much to say. But the thing is . . . " I stopped for a second to gather my courage. "The thing is . . . it's . . .

um . . . it's . . . " and then with a rush, I blurted out: "It's really hard for me to listen to you."

I looked at Frances to see how she was taking this. It was time to confront her, to tell her that she was tough to listen to because she was so self-absorbed, because she rambled so much, because she talked and talked but never listened. I had a pretty good idea this might be the source of her troubles in other relationships—with her husband, her daughter, and a few of her bridge partners. But there was no reaction at all.

I told her all this, and more. I used immediacy to share with her how I felt pushed away from her, finding it impossible to get close. I interpreted her fears of intimacy. I pointed out her lack of social skills. I confronted her resistance to looking at underlying issues. I even reflected what I sensed was her anger toward me at that moment. And I did it all in 5 minutes because I could see her foot tapping impatiently.

Frances looked at me and cocked her head, which seemed to be asking me if I was done. Was I sure there was nothing else I wanted to say? I smiled warmly at her and gestured back that she could respond now. As yet, she hadn't said a word, although I could see her lips pressed tight from the effort to restrain herself. I nodded again, indicating that I was truly done. I'd said what I had to say, what I'd wanted to say for weeks. "Go on," I prompted her, "what do you think?"

"What do I tink?" she repeated in her faint East European accent, "I tink that daughter of mine had better change her ways or there's gonna be serious trouble in that house." Then she was off again.

Incredibly, she didn't seem to have heard a single word I'd said. It was as if I were invisible, as if she were just renting my office as a place to rant and complain and whine.

Okay, I'm doing it again. I'm blaming Frances for being so difficult and ornery and uncooperative. I did such a poor job of conducting this session (and managing the case) that even now I refused to accept responsibility for our predicament. It was all *her* fault because she was ungrateful. Besides, she probably had some kind of brain disorder or attention deficit, or maybe hearing loss.

I became so frustrated and unappreciated that I spent the rest of the session retreating back into my fantasy. At the appointed moment when the session was over, I returned to announce it was time to stop. This presented its own challenges since Frances would continue talking to me as I escorted her out the door. Sometimes I'd find myself standing in the waiting room alone, realizing she was still in her chair jabbering away. Once I'd get her in the waiting room, as I closed the door, I'd hear her continuing to speak to me through the solid wood.

WHAT MADE THIS SESSION SO BAD

Like so much of therapy—for both participants—a lot of the action takes place on the inside. Perhaps I could be forgiven (or forgive myself) for mistimed confrontations designed more for my own amusement than to help my client. Frankly, I'm pretty certain that Frances treated my clumsy interventions more as an annoyance than anything else. But what haunts me the most to this day was the extent to which I surrendered my compassion.

The really scary thing about this case is that I seemed to have helped Frances anyway (or something did). Her family members provided ongoing reports about how much easier she was to deal with lately. Although Frances would never have admitted it directly, even she mentioned on occasion that she enjoyed coming to our one-way conversations. When I think about how little of myself I actually gave to this woman, I still feel ashamed.

I failed this client, and myself, by being unwilling to remain present with her. She was challenging to spend extended time with; certainly she rambled a lot; mostly, though, she was just plain scared and this was the only way she knew how to keep things together, by focusing on others, trying to control family members, and keep me as far away as possible.

Bad therapy, to me, is not only determined by the outcome, that is, whether the client leaves a satisfied customer (as Frances did). It is also not defined by how good I feel about a session (whether I think I did a good job), nor is it a function totally of our joint assessment of how well we did together since, after all, this relationship does represent a collaboration. I'd love to buy the idea that it is the client who does the work, the one who determines whether therapy is successful or not, but that lets me off the hook. There are times when I really do a lousy job because I'm not present, because I'm lazy, because I do or say stupid things. If I have a good enough relationship with the person, I can usually recover and get things back on track as I seemed to have done with Frances.

Some would say that I'm too hard on myself, that I take too much responsibility for the outcomes, and to that, I plead guilty. But it's not something I care to change. As much as I would like to shift most of the responsibility onto my clients for their work, I also accept that I have a choice about how much I want to give, how hard I want to try, how inventive I want to be, how determinedly I want to work. Perhaps I am deluding myself about having more power than is possible for a mortal being, but that's how I do this job, and this is the price I pay.

So, what did I do that was so utterly putrid, so unworthy of my professional capabilities? Let me name them.

1. I felt disrespectful and judgmental toward my client. She had hired me to understand her and instead I blamed her for being the way she was. Clients come to see us in the first place because they can't work things out on their own, nor can they find useful help from their friends and family.
2. I became lazy. I gave up. I surrendered to my boredom. I took the easy way out and cruised. I refused to remain present, with her, and instead only pretended to listen, and to care.
3. I tried to "punish" Frances for failing to entertain me, for not letting me talk, for ignoring me, for not letting me help the way I wanted to. Rather than engaging her at the level that she was at, I needed her to move more quickly. I became restless and impatient.

Even this exaggerated self-condemnation is continued evidence of my need to suffer for my sins. If truth be told, on the larger scale of things, this was hardly the disaster I am making it seem. It is because this incident was so ordinary, so apparently harmless, that I remember it as my worst session and selected it as the one to write about. It shows me at a time when I functioned most ineffectively, operating on auto-pilot. I was feeling burned out, dispirited, and tired of practicing. Not only with Frances, but with others, I would periodically leave the room in my head.

Ever since this episode, I've been curious as to how often other practitioners escape their sessions in fantasy. Just as interesting to me is where they go. To make lists? Relive a pleasant trip? Plan an adventure? Lapse into sexual fantasy? I'd guess that somewhere between 30 and 50% of the time (depending on the client and the issues discussed), most therapists have left their sessions for a period of time. This happens for a number of reasons:

1. *Boredom.* We get tired of the routines. We have heard similar stories before. The client is repeating him or herself for the umpteenth time.
2. *Threat.* What is being presented is a little too close to home. It triggers our own issues. It stirs up things that we would prefer would be left alone.
3. *Personal stuff.* There are things going on in our lives that haunt us. It is difficult to concentrate on what is going on because we are upset about something. We are feeling angry, misunderstood, confused, or aroused by a relationship. We are mulling over something that we want to do, and how we want to do it. We are undergoing some personal trauma, transition, or crisis.
4. *Laziness.* We just don't feel like investing the hard work that is needed to remain focused. It is just so easy to drift off, to get into our own

stuff, to let our concentration waver. Sometimes we are just plain depleted and tired.

With Frances, I wasn't there for her much at all. I just presented a shell that nodded occasionally, inserted a few uh-huhs, and spent most of the hour lost in my own fantasies of driving sports cars, climbing rock walls, undressing attractive women I'd seen that day, and reliving all the things I wish I'd said a little better to people I had been with earlier. I also counted the dots on the ceiling tiles, trying to estimate how many were in the room, and played imaginary piano notes with my right hand.

Is this all understandable? Sure. Forgivable? Most definitely. But for my clients' and students' sake it's important for me to remember this mediocrity so I don't settle for such laziness again.

WHAT OTHERS MIGHT LEARN

1. It isn't just when you do something dramatically stupid or graceless that you become a bad therapist, but also when you demonstrate benign neglect.
2. Being intensely self-reflective and self-critical has its benefits in promoting continued growth and learning, but also some very negative side effects related to being unforgiving of inevitable lapses, mistakes, failures, and imperfections.
3. The process of therapy is a peculiar enterprise in which both participants regularly leave the room under various circumstances when they are bored or threatened, but also when buttons are pushed, connections are made, or just as part of the normal flow of consciousness.

Doing therapy is just about the hardest mental work that anyone can do for a living (besides being an air traffic controller). Unlike others who have demanding, exacting work, we may personalize so many things that occur because they are so intensely personal. We must live with the reality that no matter how hard we study, how much training we get, how long we practice, how hard we concentrate, how much supervision we undergo, we still won't give nearly as much as our clients need, and as much as they deserve. Moreover, we will never meet our own standards of perfection. We will do good therapy and, at times, bad therapy. The thing is: Just hope you can tell the difference.

Chapter 2

JON CARLSON
Stories Without Endings

Since we began this project I have been living with the impending presence of bad therapy in every session that I do. I still see anywhere from 40 to sometimes 70 people a week and I've been doing that for 25 years.

Each day I arrive at my office early and I go down the list of people who are coming in that day and I check my own reaction to each one. I check out the people I really look forward to seeing and I wonder whose needs are going to be met in the session. Then I look at the ones I am dreading and I really think that I have to reframe this. I have to change my formulation or else I'm probably not going to be very helpful.

BEING GOOD ENOUGH

The first question I considered is probably the most provocative and riskiest; that is, something about myself as a therapist that I've never revealed before. Considering that I talk for a living, all day long, to students, supervisees, and clients, there is actually very little that I have held back. But if there is one thing it's probably that I have a lot of inferiority problems. I wonder a lot if I am good enough.

Jeffrey is surprised when he hears this from me. He tells me that he's never met anyone who appears so poised and in control in front of crowds. Here I've devoted the last 10 years to producing 100 videos of the best therapists on the planet, yet I still feel insecure inside, as if I'm not good enough to be counted among them.

I came into this whole therapy field via the back door. I trained as a schoolteacher but I never taught. Then I was trained as an elementary school counselor but I probably knew about as much about counseling as my supervisor. My supervisor knew a lot about research and teaching but he had never been a counselor before. Then I went on to doctoral

17

study (coincidently with the same advisor as Jeffrey), and rather than getting a lot of supervision, I actually became a supervisor. I had kind of moved through and hadn't gotten a lot of feedback on my work. I did it for quite a while. I would write about it and I would practice but I wasn't really sure I knew what I was doing.

But I'm sure I must have damaged other people because I would have played into some things that now, I hope, I would do differently. I think the knowledge base has changed a lot too. I went back to school to get another degree to learn how to do therapy. I figured that if one doctorate wasn't enough to make me feel competent, then perhaps another one would do it.

I was thinking that another degree would provide me with the kind of real supervision and training that I had missed the first time around. I came into this profession at a really awkward time, when credentialing and licensure were just beginning. You could really be grandfathered in via a number of other professions without having to go through the training that people go through today.

CONFRONTING INFERIORITY AND NARCISSISM

Since I have been writing about Adlerian therapy for the past 20 years, the theme of inferiority plays a big part in my thinking. I have had this wonderful opportunity to make videotapes with all of the best therapists of our time and also to put mine out there with them. Even with my doubts, I realize that I'm holding my own. I'm pleased and proud of what I do. I feel a lot better about this but it's been a process that has only happened in the last couple of years since I started to believe that I know what I am doing.

When Jeffrey came in to do his own video with me a similar phenomenon occurred. We have been watching these videos our whole lives, and now we are making them, and other therapists, some who really do seem to know what they are doing, admire our work.

Yet ironically, my biggest struggle in my career is with my own narcissism. I grew up as the youngest in a family, 8 years younger than anybody else. I was probably spoiled and felt entitled. I needed to be right. I had a pushy mother who kept pushing and pushing and pushing. I think I carry a lot of that with me today. I have to really work on that all the time.

I'm often in session with people who are my brethren, my fellow narcissists, and we get into arguments. I'm often blindsided. I'm in the middle of a power conflict with the administrator of our university right now. I'm getting a lot of support from my colleagues and I'm struggling really hard in trying to understand what it must be like to be an administrator. Sometimes in these situations I am right, but it isn't particularly helpful.

MY CASE OF BAD THERAPY

Like many of our participants, at first I had a hard time thinking of a case I wanted to present. So many of the situations where things didn't work out well occurred because I believed it was the client's fault. I did think about one example that still bothers me quite a lot. I'm not sure how to even talk about it.

I was seeing a young woman who really wanted to leave her husband. Week after week she would talk about the awful encounters she would have with him. Since I live and work in a small community, I know everyone in town. In this case, I knew the woman and her husband because they both attended the same church that I go to with my family. Actually, she was originally referred to me in the first place by the minister of our church.

My client volunteered a lot at the church and she also spent rather a lot of time talking to the minister about her problems, in addition to her sessions with me. My practice was growing at this time and my office manager came to me and wanted to know if she could get some additional help with office work. She went and hired my client to work with her. She thought that this woman could use some extra money and since she wasn't actually working for me, there wouldn't be a problem of a dual relationship. You have to remember that this was during the early 1980s when there were very different rules about what constituted inappropriate dual relationships. This case is one good example why we now have stricter ethical codes.

The woman began helping out in the office while I continued to see her in therapy. A few times her husband came in with her for couples work, although not much seemed to be working well either in the relationship or in our therapy. I don't think she wanted things to work out with her husband and I don't think he cared much either. They were both rather strong-willed people.

The wife eventually wanted out of the marriage so she moved out on her own. Then one day after they were separated, the client came in one day and said her husband was really mad and had been acting strangely. I asked her what she meant and she said that he was really concerned that she and I were having an affair. This took me completely by surprise, but because she was spending a lot of time at our office it wasn't completely out of the realm of possibility, especially if the husband had good reason to believe she was having an affair with someone. I just thought this was kind of amusing because I would never do such a thing.

During the next couple of sessions the client mentioned her husband's concern over our supposed affair. I finally asked her why her husband continued to believe this absurd rumor, and she said because she *was* having an affair, and had been doing so for quite some time, something she had never admitted before. And who might that be with, I asked her. It was with the minister!

So now I felt betrayed on multiple levels. My client had been hiding this deep, dark secret all the time I'd been seeing her, and without this critical piece of information, much of our work together was a waste of time. And then the minister of my church, the guy who referred this woman to me in the first place, was the one who was breaking up her marriage. I was so confused and angry I wasn't sure what to do. I just felt devastated.

The minister had been my mentor for many years. He had conducted marriage enrichment groups that my wife and I had attended. I knew his wife and his kids. Of course, I couldn't help but take this personally. I had totally missed what was going on.

The next thing that happened was I got a call from a lawyer soon after my client filed for divorce. Because I live in a small community, he called off the record to tell me that he was trying to talk the husband out of filing a lawsuit against me and turning me in to the Licensing Board for unethical conduct because he believed I was having sex with his wife. I was really stuck. I had confidentiality to protect so I couldn't tell the lawyer it wasn't me who was sleeping with her but her minister. In talking with my client we tried to figure out how to handle this. At this point, the therapy was no longer for her; it was really for me and my problems. She talked to her lover, the minister, about coming forward but he was a good friend of the husband too. Besides, he claimed, he was a happily married man.

Meanwhile, in the interim, the husband began seeing another therapist. My client wouldn't give me permission to talk to the minister but she agreed to try to arrange a meeting with me and the husband and the husband's therapist. She agreed that I could tell the other therapist what was gong on providing that she did not pass this information on to her client.

Fortunately, the other therapist really did some good mediation and was able to calm the husband down and try to get him to look at why their relationship didn't work. As it turned out, I wasn't defrocked of my license and I wasn't accused of improprieties, but I still have to take responsibility for creating a big part of this mess.

The husband eventually remarried, but continued to hate me for years. The minister eventually left town and moved on, as did my client. I'm not sure what happened to either one of them. I do still see the husband occasionally and he seems to have forgiven me for what he still believes was my seduction of his wife. I still can't tell him the truth.

LEARNING ABOUT BOUNDARIES

This case was a turning point for me, especially with regard to establishing clear boundaries between personal and professional relationships. Of course I should never have allowed her to be hired to work in my office in the first place. In today's climate, that must sound like a pretty stupid misjudgment but at that time this sort of thing was nothing compared to other things that were going on. This was at the height of the encounter group movement when everyone was doing whatever they wanted. I'm just very grateful that at least the lawyer and the other therapist were willing to step forward and mediate the situation.

On a more personal level, I had a lot of feelings that I couldn't talk much about. I felt pretty stymied. Thereafter, it was hard for me to go to church as I knew the minister, my friend and mentor, was a hypocrite. I was concerned about my reputation in this small community since word had leaked out that I had done some awful things, none of which were true. And worst of all—I couldn't even defend myself. Until this point in my life, I figured that people were basically trustworthy—especially members of the clergy.

A MORE RECENT SITUATION

Like so many of the people that we have interviewed, I picked a case from a long time ago as a way to distance myself from a subject that is so threatening. I'd like now to talk about another variation on the theme where I was right but it didn't help much.

I was working with a young man in his early 30s. He was an educated man and worked at the local college. He came in to see me for some relationship issues, but while talking to him it came out that he was also recovering from drug and alcohol abuse. As we talked about this history, he mentioned that he would be in recovery for the rest of his life.

Based on my own experience, I have problems with that kind of thinking. I wonder if people ought to spend their whole life, everyday, thinking about the greatest wrong that they have done to themselves. I think that is a major liability. I happened to mention to him that there was some evidence that people really could train themselves to become social drinkers. It was just an off-the-cuff kind of statement. The guy just nodded his head, but didn't say anything in response.

A few days later I got a letter from him in which he said that I was the most unprofessional person in the world and how could I possibly think that people weren't alcoholics for life? How could I ever believe that people could be taught to drink socially? He said he was never going to come back and see me again.

I think I had sent him some information as part of his termination letter. I indicated that he might want to consult the literature himself and make up his own mind about what was best for him. I also told him that this was controversial stuff but he still might find it useful. If I'm honest with myself, I have to admit as well that it was important for me to be right again, even if it wasn't useful to him.

I received a call from him and a very nice letter a couple of years later. He said that he was sorry about the way our relationship had ended, and furthermore, that he had started having a glass of wine with dinner and had been able to do so for more than a year without ill effects or losing control. This had really changed his life and he didn't really see himself as an alcoholic anymore. I thought that was pretty encouraging, and I was grateful that he took the time to let me know how he was doing. So often when clients leave, we never find out what happened and how the story ended.

A short time later I received a call that was followed up by a police officer visiting my house. The officer came by to tell me that there had been a threat against my life. He said that they planned on patrolling my street on a regular basis. What had happened was that this fellow had gone out one evening and got drunk and then he began losing control. He had lost his job and had become really down-and-out, totally irresponsible. He was eventually arrested for being out of control and when he was in detox at the local emergency room he was screaming how he was going to kill me and that it was all my fault that his life was in ruins. I got a letter from his wife basically telling me that I was the worst therapist in the world and how all of this had ruined their lives. It turned out that the only thing that he heard from me was that I gave him permission to drink as much as he wanted.

After this happened, I couldn't sleep. I kept going over in my mind what I had said to him and how he could have possibly interpreted it. I wondered what I could have done differently. It was really upsetting to me that such a spontaneous passing remark could have such a huge negative impact. Again I was right: research supported what I had said but it was totally inappropriate for this individual.

I learned after that to be very careful about the things I say to people.

At the very least, I might say to him now, "Would you be interested in knowing . . . ?" Or maybe I wouldn't bring it up at all.

So, what do I conclude from these two cases of bad therapy? If you do enough therapy, you are going to have some problems. The important thing, though, is not to keep making the same mistakes. In the past I might have said to myself that it was too bad, but it was the guy's own fault he didn't do what he was supposed to do. But it was my job to give that information in a different way, and to respect where he was coming from. Having worked with people in the 12-Step Program before, I should have known better. The saddest part for me is that I never got to talk with him. We were never able to reach closure together.

I have a lot of regret and sadness about the blessedly few failures I have encountered. They are stories without endings, and I have to live with that. So many of these cases of bad therapy have no real ending, and that's the way I want to close my chapter.

Chapter 3

PEGGY PAPP
A Public Humiliation

PEGGY PAPP is known primarily for her ground-breaking work that explores gender differences in the practice of family therapy. In her classic books, *The Process of Change* and *Family Therapy: Full Length Case Studies*, she was among the first to trace family belief systems that influence the core values of individual members. She later refined her theories in collaboration with others involved in The Women's Project to publish *The Invisible Web: Gender Patterns in Family Relationships*. Most recently, she edited a new book for marital therapists: *Couples on the Fault Line: New Directions for Therapists*.

Papp's early training was in journalism and drama, two professions she combined into a career as a Hollywood reporter of the movie scene. She later moved to New York where she pursued an acting career on stage until she decided to integrate these talents with training as a social worker. She became associated with the Ackerman Institute, practicing and writing about her unique gender-sensitive approach to helping families sort out their conflicts. She now maintains a private practice in New York as well as supervising therapists at North General Hospital.

THERE WERE A THOUSAND WITNESSES

Getting right to the point, Peggy Papp blurted out that the worst therapy session she ever did was in front of a thousand witnesses. "It's even on videotape," she said with a laugh. "I mean, how do you like that? It's one thing to fail in private and quite another to be embarrassed in public. This was at a family therapy conference in California about 8 years ago.

It was one of those live interview demonstrations and I was going to demonstrate the technique of sculpting. It is a method that I have used all over the world for many years. I ask each member of the couple or family to have a fantasy about their relationship and then act out the fantasy together. The fantasies provide a metaphorical picture of how each person experiences their relationships. The metaphors are then used as a vehicle for changing their relationship. Because the experience is nonverbal and based on symbols, images, and metaphors it is understood in every language."

We were both nodding our heads, easily imagining how brilliant and foolproof such a demonstration would be in the able hands of Peggy Papp. It would be a perfect situation for Peggy to show her best stuff—dramatic, spontaneous, with lots of opportunities to highlight her theory in action. As she had done such presentations all over the world, on every part of the globe, it made sense that she would feel so confident.

"I had had such a wonderful experience doing sculpting in many different countries. Everybody had warned me, for example, that the Japanese were stereotyped as uncommunicative and unexpressive, yet they came up with the most imaginative fantasies and were very expressive. Wherever I've done these demonstrations, people always respond well."

Papp still felt uncomfortable recalling this situation in which she believed she had failed miserably. We teased her that she could never show her face again in California. She laughed politely, but there were still the remnants of pain in her voice.

PRESSURES INSIDE AND OUT

I was working with a couple. The wife couldn't come up with a fantasy and the husband had a fantasy about a rock, which is a little difficult to sculpt." We laughed, trying to imagine the challenges of working with such a couple on stage. To make matters still worse, Papp worked within a structure that made audience participation awkward.

"Generally I get feedback from the audience. I take a break. I listen to what they say, and then I put their ideas together with mine and come up with some kind of a message that pulls everything together and makes the sculpting meaningful to the family at the end. What happened this time was that the audience was too big. I made a huge mistake by not asking for a panel, like maybe six people, who would come up and act as my consultation team. So I got too many suggestions from the audience that were irrelevant and not helpful."

With all the chaos of trying to manage the oversize audience, Papp was also feeling the negative residue from knowing she had not performed at her best with the couple. And through all this she was trying to think under a lot of pressure, both internal and external.

MISTAKES AND MISCALCULATIONS

"I just wasn't very helpful with this family." As Papp admitted her failure, she couldn't seem to get over the extent to which she had ignored her intuition for the sake of a structure that was not working.

Ordinarily, Papp does not like to get much background on families from the referring therapist. She wants to form her own impressions rather than be influenced by the biases and perceptions of others. This was the reason she had not asked for much background information on the case. "This was a major mistake because the therapist eventually told me some things about the family that were so important to know about—deaths and cutoffs in the family."

All of this came out in the analysis of the session after the interview was over. "So I compounded my embarrassment when the therapist revealed these facts after I had given this very flimsy kind of message back to the family. I just felt it was the worst session I had ever done."

It was at this point that Papp changed the subject, pleading that these events happened so long ago, she couldn't remember much more about what happened. We asked her, instead of thinking about the couple, to focus instead on what she remembered about her feelings and personal reactions to the event.

"This was an unusual experience for me because it was before a big audience. This is one reason why I felt so overwhelmed." This made perfect sense. Ordinarily, when we do lousy work, the worst thing that happens is that the client might not respond the way we would like. In many cases, we can blow some intervention or bungle a method and the client doesn't notice. But in this instance there were literally a thousand eyes and ears dissecting and analyzing Papp's every move.

"I'm always trying very hard to do my best in these situations. This sometimes works against being relaxed enough so I can really hear the family. If I were working with this couple in my private practice I would probably not have done the same thing, so that put tremendous pressure on me."

In hindsight, Papp realized how unrealistic and inappropriate it is to decide ahead of time on a treatment method before even meeting the family and hearing their story. Such a structure was eventually bound to fail.

IF I COULD DO IT AGAIN

So, we asked her, what would you have done differently? If you were to walk into that auditorium again, how would you have proceeded in a more helpful way? "First, I would have really learned a lot more from the therapist if it had come as a consultation. I would have learned all of the important background. I think this would have helped me to think more clearly. I would have focused the session differently and incorporated the historical material into the discussion. In some cases the history of the couple is not that relevant but in this case it was pivotal. I missed the boat."

It was interesting to hear how someone who speaks to large audiences for a living still feels nervous and inhibited in such circumstances. This is not surprising, of course, but reassuring that no matter how long you practice therapy, even in the most stressful of circumstances, you can never really get to the point where you can handle everything deftly that comes your way. There are therapists who think they can, but that is only because they are oblivious to the different ways they could have proceeded.

EXPECTATIONS

"I guess one thing for others to learn from this episode is that if there is any kind of outside pressure that interferes with really being with a family then the help can be compromised. For instance, sometimes I feel intimidated if a big name in the field refers somebody to me. I imagine that the family's expectations are extremely high."

We all realized that Peggy was not really talking about others' expectations but rather her own unrealistic standards of perfection. She had done public demonstrations so often that she had forgotten how difficult they can be to pull off, especially when she was wedded to a particular methodology before she even began.

"I think my emphasis on the technique overwhelmed the whole thing. The plenary was publicized as a demonstration of this technique and there was a great deal of interest in it. I was obliged to demonstrate it. Otherwise, I probably wouldn't have chosen to use it at this particular time with this couple."

We were reminded of how often we had fallen into a similar trap. We remain vested in a particular treatment strategy or plan, so much so that we don't pay close attention to the dismal results.

WHY WAS I SO BAD?

We asked Papp what happened when she processed the whole episode with the audience.

"I didn't."

"You didn't?"

"No, I was too distraught. I felt terrible that I hadn't given more help to the couple. They had agreed to expose themselves to a huge audience and were expecting big results. I feel I let them down. There wasn't time to process things and I was glad of that. We were under a big time pressure, so actually after the therapist who had been working with the family had given me all this information the whistle blew and the bell rang and it was time for them to go to the next session. Even if there had been time I don't think I could have done a good job of processing it as I myslef didn't understand what had gone wrong."

Here Papp touched on a very important point that can often make bad therapy experiences linger far beyond the point where such reflection is constructive. It seems crucial in such situations to have the opportunity to make sense of what happened, to figure out what went wrong, and what could have been done instead. It is one thing to be bad, and quite another to not understand why.

"I kept thinking to myself, what happened? Why didn't I do something else? Why didn't I do this, why didn't I do that? What else could I have done? That was the kind of processing that went through my mind. And I kicked myself for months after that. Why didn't I do this, I should have thought of that, I should have done this."

If these self-punitive thoughts weren't so familiar to us, we would be surprised by the irrational expectations of perfection. Even after decades of practice, endless hours of supervision, personal therapy, intensive training, even teaching this stuff to others, we still share Papp's high standards that can never be met. Rather than apologizing for this, we take pride in our excessive achievement that was bred into us as children, part of the legacy that led us into therapy in the first place.

We are not trying to let Papp off the hook, but although she may have thought she had totally blown the interview, the family and the audience may very well have believed it was brilliant, or at least acceptable. We know from our own experiences of being in an audience that we feel so humbled and inadequate watching the masters at work even when they are not nearly at their best.

"Well," Papp reassured us, "in this case I doubt that would be possible."

We still challenged her assumptions. So often we do demonstrations, sometimes pretty lousy ones, yet we hear afterwards how marvelous they were and how satisfied people were with the results. Maybe it is a self-fulfilling prophesy or the positive benefits of a reputation, but sometimes there is little correlation between how we think we did and the assessment of others.

"The conference organizers did send me the ratings," Papp admitted. "They weren't that bad really. There was one person who said it was the best session ever. That's one tenth of a percent, not very high, is it? I think people could sense my discomfort about the way things ended with not much meaningful feedback to the couple."

HUMILITY AND COURAGE

Some years ago Peggy Papp wrote a foreword to Coleman's *Failures in Family Therapy* (1985). In this essay she talked about the humility and the courage it takes to talk about failures. She said: "Failure is inevitably followed by haunting reflections, lingering regrets, and a wish to petition the gods for more wisdom" (p. xi).

We asked her how she felt about this statement many years later. How did she feel it applied to the honest and open disclosures that she had just shared with us?

"I still think it's very important to do that because I think particularly when you make a lot of presentations and you have written books and you have a reputation, people automatically assume that most of your sessions go like on the videotapes and that you always know the answers and that you are always sensitive and wise. It's just not true. I also think that human behavior is so mysterious and unpredictable that if you are not humble about it you are bound to be insensitive to a lot of the dilemmas and predicaments that people are facing. It takes wisdom sometimes, not techniques and approaches to be helpful to people. It takes a kind of real understanding about human suffering."

Peggy paused for a moment, unsure of what she was trying to say. She sounded perfectly clear to us, and more than a little wise, but she seemed to want some encouragement and support from her listeners. We were eager to offer it and anxious to hear more.

"Talking about humility," she continued, "I am actually in awe of human endurance. I took a new job in January. I am working at a hospital in Harlem teaching psychiatric residents to do family therapy. This man came in the other day, a father, and he is at the bottom of the barrel economically and educationally, I think in nearly every way. He is without a job and he has a physical disability. He is illiterate. He has been in jail. He has difficulty controlling his violent temper. He has been a drug addict. He overcame that and he has overcome alcoholism. But he sits there and when I ask him what he would like to gain from this session he says 'I want to be a good father to my son and I want to improve my relationship with Betty (his companion).' Where does he get the strength to keep hoping for something better?

"I'm in awe of that spirit. So, when I talk about humility, that is the kind of thing I mean. This man had been described in the clinic before as being resistant and uncommunicative—missing appointments—categorized as being very difficult. Nobody understood why it's difficult for him to get to his sessions; I think they really missed it. That's why I'm talking about humility."

UPON REFLECTION

One of the interesting side effects of a provocative conversation is that the dialogue continues in our heads long after the talk has ended. We discovered that we were not the only ones who kept thinking about public and private humiliations, and the lessons learned from such painful encounters, when we received a postscript from Peggy in the mail. She had been thinking about the way she trains new therapists, emphasizing respect for clients' cultural differences, and this reminded her of another example of bad therapy that still haunted her.

"I was seeing a couple at the Ackerman Institute in which the wife was English and the husband was from the Middle East. The wife was pregnant with their first child. She had suffered severe bouts of depression all her life and she was afraid she might experience postpartum depression that would interfere with her caring for the baby. The husband's mother wanted to come and stay with them during the birth but the wife objected, saying she wanted the initial experience of the baby to be between just the two of them. The husband was afraid of offending his mother, but reluctantly agreed to a compromise; his mother would come to this country but live separately until they had time to adjust to the baby and then she would join them in their home. At the time, this seemed to be an agreeable solution to both of them."

Papp went on to discuss other issues with the couple, including the husband's language difficulties, his limited job options, concerns about money, and ongoing conflicts over household responsibilities. They covered a lot of ground in a brief period of time and Peggy felt that things were going well. Surprisingly, however, the husband abruptly dropped out of therapy with no explanation other than saying it wasn't helpful. This was very puzzling to Papp who spent considerable time reviewing the case with colleagues to figure out what went wrong.

"Several months later," Papp explains, "the couple sent an announcement of the birth of their baby girl. I responded with a congratulatory card and said that I would very much enjoy seeing the baby and talking to them in a follow-up session. During the course of our conversation, I asked the husband to tell me more about his reasons for withdrawing from therapy. He then informed me that I had not understood his feelings about his mother. In his country, it is traditional for the grandmother to be present at the birth of grandchildren. He decided to see a therapist from his own culture who would understand this."

Papp realized that she had been so focused on protecting the wife that she had failed to understand and acknowledge the husband's deep commitment to his mother and family traditions. The compromise that had been reached was not helpful because she had not explored the meaning of their experiences in enough depth. She had made the one mistake that she stresses so strongly with her supervisees: work within the particular cultural context of each person and respect those beliefs. "That is why," Peggy concluded, "training is such a continuous process."

Chapter 4

ARNOLD A. LAZARUS
A Huge Dose of Humility

ARNOLD LAZARUS had been at one time a staunch behavior therapist. In fact, he was the one to coin that term. He later embraced a far more integrative model in *Behavior Therapy and Beyond* that combined his early behavioral inclinations with cognitive therapy and other contributions. His trademark multimodal therapy thus became one of the most enduring systematic approaches that was both comprehensive and eclectic in orientation, providing practitioners with a model for assessment and treatment planning that includes all facets of human experience.

Among his 17 or so published books are the classic presentations of his theory such as *The Practice of Multimodal Therapy* and *Brief but Comprehensive Psychotherapy: The Multimodal Way*. More recently, Lazarus has written several popular books for the public applying his methods in *I Can If I Want To, Marital Myths Revisited: A Fresh Look at Two Dozen Mistaken Beliefs About Marriage*, and *The 60 Second Shrink: 101 Strategies for Staying Sane in a Crazy World*.

Lazarus has spent most of his career as a faculty member at Rutgers University, New Brunswick, New Jersey, where he is now Distinguished Professor Emeritus. Since the early 1970s he has been one of the most influential thinkers writing about the importance of practicing integrative, pragmatic therapy. In his distinctive South African accent, Arnie Lazarus uses a formal array of syntax that belies his wit and irreverence. He had made detailed notes about each of the questions we might ask and organized his thoughts into a steady flow of ideas. There was actually very little we had to do to lead the conversation since poor performance is an entity that he has long managed to avoid.

THE FALLIBILITY THING

We began the conversation by thanking him for his time and willingness to help us with the project.

"A pleasure," he said. "Of course if I make a complete fool of myself, my career is over and my license will be revoked."

"Well," Jon replied without skipping a beat, "that's what we're hoping for."

This banter set the tone for what was to follow. Lazarus speaks so expressively and poetically that it was sometimes difficult to interrupt the flow of his thoughts; it was far more fun just to let him go where he wanted.

Departing from the scheduled script, the first question we asked was what he was thinking about while anticipating the conversation. Actually, we thought about asking how he felt about it but remembered his solid cognitive therapy leanings. Lazarus paused for only a moment before he replied. "The whole subject strikes me as interesting because I know how cagey so many of our colleagues can be. So often we hear about their great results and fantastic cures, but only in a very few instances of errors or failures or shortcomings." We couldn't have agreed with him more. We prompted him with relish, sensing that he was fully open to being as honest and open as we could have dreamed.

"So that's why when I first heard from you guys I said to myself this would be a very good thing to be involved with. I was pleasantly surprised to see that so many of our esteemed colleagues had signed up. I am really curious to read the book when it is done and see what the other people said. I think there should be a prize for the biggest bimbo."

We all laughed. "So," Jeffrey ventured, "What about yourself? What are some times in which you have been willing to share those parts of your work?"

"I believe very much in the fallibility thing. I really credit Albert Ellis for that. He's the one who first got me onto 'Let's be fallible, and let's not pretend that we are some kind of deity who never makes mistakes. Let's help people to learn from mistakes.'

"I remember one case in point that just shows how easy it is to beguile people. I was doing a one-way mirror session and my class was watching. For whatever reason I was having an off day. I felt that everything that I was doing just sucked. If I were watching one of the students doing this I would have suggested that he or she go into another line of work. When the session was over, the class and I had a little postmortem and discussed what had transpired. The students astutely said, 'Why didn't

you pick up on that point? And why did you say this and not say that?'
So I delivered a range of unbelievable rationalizations."

We were listening to the story, feeling his shame vicariously. When someone does point out a shortcoming we often act as though it was intentional. When we do something stupid or thoughtless, we do our best to cover our tracks.

Lazarus reported that his students were becoming more and more depressed. They were looking at his behavior, comparing it to what they might have done, and feeling certain that they were more clueless about how to do good therapy than they ever believed. Finally, Arnie decided that he had been deceiving them quite enough and readily admitted that he was absolutely awful in the session. He honestly owned his blunders and reassured the students that their criticisms and observations were all extremely accurate.

Lazarus emphasized that he considered it very important to admit clinical lapses and blunders. "On the other hand there are times when you are with a client and you feel that you are absolutely brilliant. It is so incredible what you are doing and the pity is that nobody can see it. The entire world, even the peasants in the paddies in China should be looking up at huge TV screens to appreciate your brilliance. But during those other times when we are being a lot less than wonderful, we are delighted that nobody can see how we are really screwing up and we are grateful for and comforted by the privacy. I think we can all relate to that."

Indeed we could. For a moment we were all quiet, silent in our re-membrances of past mistakes, many of which were never discovered. The truth of the matter is that so much of the time our clients are so preoccupied with their own stuff that they don't even notice when we do bad work. They are so obsessed with their own imperfections that they fail to notice those of their helpers. And when clients do comment on our blunders, we joke that they should be held to confidentiality as much as we are.

"That's right," Lazarus kidded back. "If you tell anyone how crappy I was today, I'll deny it. On some admittedly rare occasions I sometimes feel there are sessions that are so bad that I should pay the client some damages. I'm happy to say again this rarely happens, but I think we have all had those experiences. We have our off days."

Given his meticulous, deliberate, controlled, and intentional style, it is difficult to imagine any time in which Arnold Lazarus is less than perfect. Before we could follow this theme some more, and it was definitely one that intrigued us, Lazarus led us back to the planned agenda. He had made some notes and wanted to proceed in the same orderly, logical manner as his signature multimodal therapy.

A LIST OF TRANSGRESSIONS

"I believe your first question was about what I think is bad therapy. A number of things come to mind, but the first one is when the therapist lacks empathy. There is no compassion." Referring to his notes, Lazarus mentioned other manifestations of ineffective help. He had a list of lapses that he considered especially deleterious, such as when therapists don't hear their clients, when they constantly answer questions with other questions, when they engage in labeling, consistently misread the client, or employ malignant interpretations. "It's bad therapy when therapists ridicule clients or insult them or use any kind of destructive criticism. Failing to use empirically supported techniques when relevant is another prime example of bad therapy."

The list continued for another minute or so, giving clear indications of what Lazarus considered good and bad treatment. Not surprisingly for someone who has devoted his life to supporting his methods with sound reasoning and research support, Lazarus's ideas were quite consistent with standard practices. What struck us as most surprising were his remarks about the negative effects that occur when therapists are cold or aloof. We readily agreed with him, of course.

Again trying to keep the focus as personal as possible, Lazarus was asked about his own behavior. "Among the items on this list, which ones do you violate the most?"

"I would think that there are times when I am less engaged or not as concerned as might be called for." There is that old compassion issue slipping in again. "It's like that scene in the movie, *Analyze This*, when Billy Crystal says to the client: 'Will you get a life and get out of my face.' That's the feeling I have sometimes and I realize that's not good for the client."

Although we couldn't actually see one another during a three-way conference call, we were both nodding our heads in agreement. This is one of the most difficult challenges for each of us, not only to act empathetically but also to really feel that way inside. So often, that critical, judgmental voice in the back of our heads starts whispering forbidden thoughts about how much we dislike someone we are helping or how impatient we feel with what we perceive is a lack of progress. During those times when we have seen 8, 9, or even 10 clients in a day, it is even more difficult to concentrate on remaining caring; under such circumstances we have sometimes found ourselves functioning on autopilot.

Lazarus owned to his own self-critical proclivities and how he was continuing to work on them. He learned many years ago to be more gentle and less threatening when he gave clients honest feedback on their behavior. Nevertheless, this remained an area in which he continued to monitor himself carefully.

ON TO SPECIFICS

The subject next turned to a specific case that stood out as among the most memorable bad sessions that Lazarus had ever done. The one he selected occurred over 20 years ago.

"This was a fellow in his 40s who was in therapy because he had lost three jobs in eight months and he had reluctantly agreed to seek help at his wife's urging. He came into the therapy very skeptical and hostile and attacking. That never changed.

"'You psychologists are a bunch of losers,' he'd say to me. 'What a motley tribe you are and you are half-crazy yourselves.'" That was a typical refrain. Initially, I tried using paradox to deflect his criticism. I would agree with him and say, 'Let me tell you about some of the idiots in my profession that you don't even know about.' That helped me to avoid being too defensive.

"I remember one time we had a session. . . . "

Lazarus stopped for a moment, and then admitted, "You know, I never liked the guy. I couldn't really warm to this fellow. My own sort of covert thinking was, 'Hell, I'm not surprised this guy has lost jobs. I'm amazed he ever got one.' Then I met his wife a few times. She was such a very nice person and I wondered what she was doing with a jerk like him. I used to ask her if she was some sort of a masochist.

"One day in the middle of a session, I started to use self-disclosure, saying to him, 'I want to share something with you about me in this regard.' He stopped me and said, 'Is this for your benefit or mine?'" This comment stopped Lazarus in his tracks. He thought about the question for a moment and then felt fully satisfied that his disclosure was clearly for the man's benefit and not self-indulgent in any way. Nevertheless, he decided to use this moment to challenge the man a bit.

"This is for your benefit," Lazarus told him. "But let's say that this was for my benefit. Let's say I was going to take one minute out of your hour for me. What's so terrible about that?"

"That's fine," the guy agreed, "but just be sure you deduct it from the bill." Lazarus shook his head, still incredulous at how irritating this man could be. "Holy Moly, is there any mystery as to why this guy has difficulty with friends and marriage and jobs? I suggested to him that this attitude might not be the best way to go through life. But anyway, I was growing more and more and more irritated by this fellow."

We chuckled. Again, each of us was reliving our own traumatic memories working with someone like this who got underneath our skins.

"So what happened in this very bad session—one in which I was seeing this guy and his wife—was that he went on the attack and began to light into me and then he went after his wife. Now I don't know why I responded this way because I can usually handle aggression pretty well, so I can't explain why I saw red."

It was hard to imagine a perfectly controlled guy like Arnold Lazarus ever losing control. We wondered what that would look like. When we've seen him on stage or in videos demonstrating his theory, it appears as if nothing could possibly ruffle him. He proceeds from one step to another, endlessly patient with the people he sees.

"I just lost it," Lazarus said. "I went ballistic in a major way." Again we tried to picture him in the midst of a rant, when he clarified that he wasn't exactly kicking and screaming. In his irritation, Lazarus told the patient that he was a really reprehensible guy. He turned to the man's wife and said, "I don't know why you put up with this guy. I mean he is the most royal pain in the neck."

Lazarus admitted that this was by no means a calculated therapeutic confrontation. He just lost control. "I was not a therapist. I stopped being a therapist at that point and I came across purely as a crazy fellow going for this guy's jugular. I've often thought back to this case, always with a certain amount of shame and chagrin because I don't think I've ever really blown up at anybody like this in all the years I've practiced. There have been times when I have said something like, 'Gee, you know you really are beginning to bore me because you have given me the same story 14 times. What is new here today?' But this is said without rancor. When I think back to that session where I lost it, I feel so much shame and humiliation that I want to kick myself. I'm surprised that this guy didn't report me to the licensing board or something. After that session I never saw or heard from them again."

"You must have cured them, huh?"

"I cured them like chunks of ham! I have always hung my head in shame when I think back to this case."

A SIMPLE CASE OF COUNTERTRANSFERENCE

We wondered what it was about this particular individual that got underneath the skin of the usually imperturbable Arnold Lazarus. Having given the case tremendous thought over the years, he was quick to answer that it was all the putdowns, the carping criticism, the way he treated his wife, that just bothered him.

"Now I suppose the smart thing to do was maybe to refer this guy to someone else because he was really pulling my chain. But I couldn't really think of anyone I hated enough to refer this guy to." Lazarus then went on to say: "In fact, there is a colleague I have who works about 5 or 6 miles down the road and for several years I have referred all the toughest or worst cases to him. This guy loves them. The tougher the better. And he does wonderful work with them."

This got Lazarus thinking about other difficult clients and how they sometimes responded very differently to other therapists. We thought back to previous research we'd been involved in with so-called difficult clients. One conclusion was that there really are no such things—all clients are really doing the best they can—just doing their jobs coping in the only way they know how. Instead of difficult clients there are really only difficult therapists, meaning those who are so rigid that they are unwilling or unable to make the necessary adjustments in order to make contact with some folks, or who are reluctant to make judicious referrals.

"So," Lazarus wondered aloud, "why did this man get to me on that particular day? I don't know. Perhaps there are just times, for whatever reason, that our own life problems place us in a vulnerable state."

Lazarus continued to verbalize his thoughts about the question, then ventured that the guy reminded him of a bully who beat him up in high school. A simple case of countertransference? It certainly made sense. And again each of us retreated into his own memories about those clients who consistently get underneath his skin.

WHAT WAS LEARNED

We wondered how this particular blunder changed things afterwards. What fascinated us so much about these cases was not what happened but how these master therapists used the experiences to improve their skills and advance their theories.

"I have often made resolutions," Arnie said. "In this instance I told myself, 'I'll never do that again'. That's how I quit smoking in 1972. I just said 'I will never have another cigarette.' So I just told myself that I will never blow up at a patient again. That was stated with full determination. Once I make that sort of a resolution I stick to it. Since then, when some people have hit some buttons I may have come close to blowing up but I have always stopped short of losing control."

We followed up this point by asking him about other injunctions that he had followed as a result of learning from his mistakes. Several examples immediately came to mind.

"One of the tendencies that I used to have was to move in too quickly without getting the full picture. I would be thinking that I've got it but I didn't have it. I would shoot off my mouth before I had obtained all the relevant facts. So I learned to check, check, double check, before moving in. This is like the good old admonishment about not making premature interpretations, but I'm talking of it in a different context. You have to really validate what's being said so that you can be sure that you are on target. I'm pretty sure there are some other therapists we both know who don't have that injunction. Many times I've seen some of these people jump to conclusions after less than a minute, and they almost always miss the point. They hadn't heard their clients. They hadn't asked the relevant questions. They didn't even realize they were way off base."

Lazarus made the point that he had learned a lot by watching supposedly good therapists do very bad therapy. He'd had a number of negative role models who had helped him to remember what not to do in his work.

WHAT OTHERS COULD LEARN

Speaking of well-known therapists who don't practice what they preach, Arnie's voice took on even greater passion. "I think that the first things these people need is a big dose of humility. I've listened to therapists imply that they're using an advanced science or they have X-ray vision or something. We all need a lot more humility.

"The other thing that is my passion at the moment is related to a book I'm doing on dual relationships. I want to rip into these rigid boundaries that clinicians set out under the guise of risk management. Therapists are so terrified by licensing boards that when there is an opportunity to be a human being they frequently don't take it.

"I am with a client at 11:00 in the morning and it's approaching noon. We're onto something pretty important so I say to him, 'Listen, I'm running down to the deli to pick up a sandwich for lunch. I have a 1:15 appointment so why don't we continue, grab some sandwiches, head up back here? No extra fee of course.' Now what is wrong with that? "But no, many would say that is a dual relationship. If the relationship is as important as everyone contends, then why destroy it with rigidity and sterility?"

Lazarus cautioned that there should be limits to this sort of thing, that client safety should always be protected, but he wondered why so many therapists were afraid of their own impulses. We agreed with him and remarked that the boundaries put in place are there more for the therapist's safety than that of the client. This reminded Lazarus of a story that we just knew was going to be amusing.

"I was having dinner with a very attractive woman one evening," he began. "She happened to be a client of mine. A guy who I know from the State Licensing Board comes by the table and says hello to me. I do the right thing; I don't want to breech confidentiality so I don't introduce him to my dinner companion. This would be the normal social thing to do so he brashly asks me who the woman is. She answered without a pause, 'My name is so-and-so. I'm Dr. Lazarus's client.'

The member of the licensing board, a staunch psychoanalyst, then looked at Lazarus with a cold stare and said with menace in his voice, "You'll be hearing from me." Then he stalked away.

A few minutes after Lazarus got home the phone rang. Sure enough, it was the Board member. He read Lazarus the appropriate sections from the Code of Ethics that had been violated and then demanded an explanation.

"Oh, this wasn't a social date," Lazarus answered him calmly. "This was a therapy session." Lazarus had expected to hear from this person and had asked his client if she would allow him to reveal a few facts about her if he did indeed call. She was quite happy to give him the go ahead. So Lazarus said: "The problem here is that this lady has had some anorexic problems and some fears of eating in public places and this is what we in the trade call in vivo desensitization."

The analyst was not amused. "You behaviorists should all be run out of town," he said. Then he hung up.

"That's a fairly typical fear that these people on licensing boards instill," Lazarus said. "You can't just practice defensively. A good clinician takes risks and if you are going to really cover your butt all the time I think clients are going to be cheated."

WE NEED MORE FALLIBILITY

Lazarus remembered that one of the questions on our original outline asked him to name some specific examples of his ineptitude. "I should probably mention that I have noticed I've become less patient over the years. I think that in my younger years I was more patient. I now begin to feel impatient and this may spill over. I don't think this is necessarily a good thing."

We found that observation interesting since normally patience is associated with becoming more experienced and aging. Lazarus disagreed, and admitted that as he has gotten older, he hasn't had the patience for some things anymore.

"I was doing a cotherapy session with my son who's some 29 years younger than I am. I was sitting there feeling bored and impatient and I was so impressed that my son was so supportive and making all the right moves. I was thinking, yeah, I used to do that. I think that my fuse has grown shorter."

Lazarus became even more reflective as he mused about the value of confessing mistakes. He thought that we'd all be better off if master therapists would step down off their pedestals and show more fallibility. He noted that therapists so often try to cover up their blunders and deny their mistakes.

"In the postdoctoral group I currently teach we often discuss blunders we have made, why we should not hide them, and what we learn from these mistakes. We meet about once a month and have these really very open discussions. I am quick to say, 'Look, I really think I screwed up here and there.'"

This sort of modeling has encouraged the other therapists in his supervision group to talk about their own doubts and fears and imperfections. It is one of the things about his work that makes him feel most proud. The conversation came to a close with Lazarus's curiosity about how disclosing other contributors had been. He had his doubts that many of his colleagues would be very willing to share their mistakes openly and honestly. We told him that he would be very surprised.

Chapter 5

VIOLET OAKLANDER
If I Learned Something,
Then I Can Forgive Myself

VIOLET OAKLANDER is one of the most sought-after teachers and supervisors for therapists who work with children. Based in Santa Barbara, California, she travels all over the world doing workshops on methods for working with children and adolescents. Her book, *Windows to Our Children*, demonstrates her unique Gestalt approach combined with other expressive techniques. She has also completed a number of training tapes that demonstrate child therapy in action.

During our conversation with her about some of the children she has tried but failed to help, we could hear genuine sadness and regret in her voice, as if, somehow, she was reliving the disappointments all over again. Although she was grateful that she had not had that many real failures in her work, there was one case that stood out above all the others and still haunted her to this day.

IF NOT HELPFUL TO THE CLIENT, THEN HELPFUL TO ME

The case that Violet wanted to talk about—or would rather *not* think about but had agreed to discuss—was one in which she learned a lot about how she works. "It may have not been good for the client, but it certainly helped me. I regret that it happened the way it did but I didn't know any better at the time. I just did the best I could."

Oaklander explained that when she did workshops, she presented a lot of successful cases that demonstrated her method. The participants, though, were always asking her to talk about her failures as well, especially since they wanted to feel reassured that they were not alone in their imperfections. Whether she decided to present such an example of bad therapy or not, this was the one case that most came to mind.

"This was a boy who was 16 years old. His father brought him to see me. Until recently, the boy had lived with his mother for many years. His mother was a raging alcoholic who was not involved in any recovery effort. Finally the father fought and got custody of the boy. He was a policeman and he had been on some sort of sensitivity training as part of his job that gave him the idea of bringing the boy into therapy."

Violet next reviewed the list of presenting complaints, many of them physical in nature. The boy had chronic stomachaches and was eventually diagnosed with ulcers. He was also very passive and quiet, very restricted in the ways he expressed himself. In addition, he had skipped a lot of school in order to go surfing with his friends.

"This was about the only thing the boy ever did," Violet said. "He didn't have many friends. Yet he was a very, very cooperative child, just like a lot of kids who might have come from an alcoholic family, especially as an only child. I realized from some of the things the boy told me later that he had helped take care of his mother a lot. He was always feeling that he had to take care of her. He actually didn't want to leave her because he worried about how she would do without him."

Oaklander explained that the boy was a little afraid of his father so he had agreed to live with him so father wouldn't be disappointed in him. Oaklander found the father a nice sort of guy, but his policemanlike style could be abrupt at times. Actually, it was not so much that the boy was afraid of his father as he desperately didn't want to disappoint him. It was for this reason that the boy attended the sessions, and appeared cooperative, even though it was obvious he would rather not have come.

"I saw him for about 6 weeks. He came in once a week and he would do anything I would tell him. He would draw. He would work with clay. In the course of all this, a lot of stuff came out about his mother and how he could never bring friends over to the house because she was drunk. He became very emotional several times. I felt that this was incredible. We were doing some great work together."

We were waiting for the other shoe to drop, knowing that things were not as they seemed. It was one of the most disorienting parts of our jobs that the times we think we are doing our best work may, in fact, be quite useless.

Sure enough, right in the midst of their excellent progress, the boy came in and announced that he refused to return for any more therapy. "I was really shocked by this because I thought that we had been doing this great work. So I asked him why he didn't want to return.

"I don't like the way I feel," the boy said simply.

"What do you mean by that?" Oaklander asked him, puzzled by his explanation.

"I feel things. And I don't like it. I don't want to feel what I am feeling."

"Can you give me an example of this?" Oaklander pressed him further, still puzzled by his explanation.

"Well," the boy said hesitantly, "one day the teacher criticized me about something and then I started to cry right in the classroom."

"Go on," Violet encouraged him.

"And then the other day a guy I wanted to be friends with said something to me that made me kind of mad and I yelled at him. I don't want to do that. I don't like this stuff. I like the way it was before when I didn't feel anything."

Oaklander tried to explain to the boy what happens in therapy when you open up your feelings, how it hurts for a little bit, but then it gets better if you stick with it. She told him about how dealing with his feelings was a way to get healthy, and to stay that way. She told him how his stomachaches, ulcers, and other physical problems were the result of holding his feelings in. Yet in spite of how persuasive she tried to be, the boy was determined not to return for more sessions.

"I called his father," Oaklander said. "He was also very puzzled by what had happened. He admitted that he couldn't make the kid return. The boy wouldn't explain why to his father and I felt I couldn't tell his father what he had told me. I felt very uncomfortable about the whole situation."

WE WENT TOO FAST

After giving the matter considerable thought, Oaklander decided that she had bungled the pace of the therapy. "I had gone much too fast with him and I just hadn't paced the sessions. I had just pushed him—it didn't feel like I pushed him—but that's really what I did. I just kept going further and further and pushing him and pushing him and all these things would come out. It was like he lost control over himself and I certainly didn't help him feel any control over anything. I thought a lot about this. I learned a lot about pacing sessions and being careful, particularly with a child with his background."

One of the things that bothered Oaklander the most about this case, besides acknowledging her overeagerness to move forward, was that she never learned what happened to the child afterwards. She thinks about him and wonders how he is doing. She tries to picture what he's doing today. But she never heard a thing about what happened. She has to live with that uncertainty.

"I try to comfort myself that whatever we did together might have been helpful to him, but I am really not sure about that."

ANOTHER CASE OF UNCERTAINTY

Since this first case was one that Oaklander sometimes brought up in her workshop as an illustration of when things go wrong, we decided to dig a little deeper just as she had tried to do with her client. We asked her about another instance of bad therapy that she'd be willing to talk about.

"I don't know if it was bad therapy or not," Violet said with real sadness in her voice, "but there was another kid. He was 13 and he was doing very badly in school. He actually wouldn't go to school a lot; he would run off. His mother brought him in and she was very angry with him.

"The boy made a pretty good connection with me in the beginning. I asked him what he did when he ran off and he said he went down to the harbor and talked to the fishermen and they sometimes let him get in their boats and he would help them fish. That is what he really liked to do. It was the only time he showed any energy when he talked, since otherwise he was pretty restricted."

Oaklander quickly realized that this was a kid who would not be very emotionally expressive, nor would he be willing to do much projective work. So instead they spent their time talking about his interests, mostly about fishing, which was a subject he knew a lot about.

She had not been seeing the boy very long before his mother came in one day and said she wanted to talk about how things were going.

"What I think you need to do," Oaklander told the mother, "is to write a note to the school and tell them that you are going to allow your son to be excused from school." She felt that the boy could use a few mental health days to go fishing. Perhaps if he was given permission to go to the harbor on occasion he might be more inclined to go to school.

While Oaklander and the mother mulled over this idea, she considered that the boy seemed to have a number of learning disabilities that were making school far more challenging than it needed to be. She wondered if getting the kid some help with his learning problems might make a difference. "The mother said she couldn't possibly do that," Oaklander recounted. "Then she got so angry with me that she stopped the boy's therapy right then and there." Oaklander stopped for a moment, as if to gather herself for the part that came next.

"It was about a month later," Oaklander continued in a voice choked with emotion, "that the mother called me to say that her son had hanged himself. She said she wished she had listened to me. Since then, I've always wondered about what I could have done or said so that she would have listened to me. I don't know if it would have helped him or not, but I always wondered about what I had missed."

WHEN UNDERSTANDING IS NOT ENOUGH

Although Oaklander found some relief in that the mother did not in any way blame her for the outcome, she still felt there was something else she could have done, even though she was still not sure what that might have been. At the time, she felt like she really understood him. She felt they had a good relationship.

"I wasn't able to help the mother understand what was going on and get her to be on his side, our side. I try to do that a lot with parents. Maybe I didn't support her enough so that then she could be on his side. I always felt that I didn't go far enough. I missed something doing that."

This was a case that Violet does not talk about, mostly because the regret still lingers and because she still hasn't figured out what really happened. "I know sometimes I will be so much the child's advocate that I might forget to listen to the parent, to honor the parent. This had been a very hard-working single mother who didn't get any support and she was just exasperated and at her wits end and the school was always calling her. She did bring him in and that was something, yet I somehow missed the boat there with her. I think that is something one has to pay attention to."

So, we asked her, what could you have done instead? What more could you have tried? What was so frustrating about this case to Oaklander was that she really did not know, even now. There are so many clients we see like this, some we have failed and some we have helped, but we can't be certain what happened. We don't know what made a difference. We don't understand what went wrong, or what went right for that matter. Sure, we have our theories, our explanations, our hypotheses, but ultimately, these are only possibilities based on such limited available data.

"If I could do it all over again," Violet mused, "I would probably have done more work with the mother so she felt honored and respected. I could have been more empathetic to what she was going through. It is not helpful to the child if we antagonize the parents, or if we criticize them. Some parents are not ready to hear things that we tell them. And I think where I went wrong is that his mother felt criticized by me."

WHAT WAS LEARNED

We asked Oaklander what stood out to her most from both of these cases. What did she learn? She returned to the first case of the boy who was afraid of his feelings. "I shouldn't get so caught up in my success in what I'm doing and instead pay more attention to how children are responding. I know that children cannot actually handle a lot of expression of feelings all at one time the way that adults can. Children are much more vulnerable that way, they don't have enough ego strength or self-support to take all the feelings in. Often children will take care of themselves by breaking contact. They say they don't want to do it anymore. With a child with his background, I needed to be more alert about not pushing him too hard. Ever since that case, I have handled this differently."

Both examples Oaklander supplied represented times when she was doing some solid work with her clients, yet things went bad because of one important facet she ignored—the power of the parents. She had good relationships with the children, yet missed an important feature that ultimately led to the failure.

"Parents take their kids out of therapy when it's not time, or it's too soon." Violet sighed, realizing the futility of some cases where she had so little control over what parents may do. "We do what we can do. We just go as long as we can, and when we can't do anymore, we can't. Maybe that sounds too simple. It's not always quite like that."

TO BE MORE FORGIVING

We couldn't help but notice how forgiving Oaklander was of her mistakes and so we asked her how she managed that. "I think that if I can say I learned some things that I can apply to other kids or situations, then I can forgive myself. I don't become too hard on myself for those things. I have regrets, and I feel bad, and then I can learn. I don't beat myself up."

As the conversation came to an end, Violet teased us that this experience was kind of serious and disturbing. "You said we were going to have fun!"

Chapter 6

RICHARD SCHWARTZ
The Critical Parts of Me

As the title of this chapter implies, DICK SCHWARTZ looks at the different parts that make up an individual, as well as the family system to which he or she belongs. In his internal family systems model, he combines traditional systemic thinking with a broader base that encompasses cultural, political, and intrapsychic facets.

Schwartz is the author of several books that describe his unique approach, including *Internal Family Systems Therapy*. He has also written several books that synthesize theory and research, including *Metaframeworks: Transcending the Models of Family Therapy, Handbook of Family Therapy Training and Supervision, The Mosaic Mind: Empowering the Tormented Selves of Abuse Survivors,* and the popular text, *Family Therapy: Concepts and Methods.*

Schwartz is a faculty member at Northwestern University's Family Institute and consults through his Center for Self Leadership in Oak Park, Illinois.

A DIFFERENT TAKE ON TRANSFERENCE

Among the various contributors to failures in therapy, Schwartz began our dialogue by mentioning the way that some practitioners pathologize their clients. "They use the DSM [Diagnostic and Statistical Model] as a kind of Bible and see people through that lens. A lot of what happens after that becomes self-fulfilling. I work a lot with survivors of sex abuse. Many of them come into my office having been labeled in the past as *borderline personality* or *multiple personality* or *heavy depression*. People who carry the label *borderline*, for example, are dreaded by therapists. The therapist's protectiveness triggers parts in the client that get into these escalating vicious circles that often lead to trouble. I don't have these struggles because I don't make those presumptions about people when they come in."

We asked Dick to explain his approach further, one that avoids the use of traditional diagnostic labels and focuses on labeling relevant parts of the self. "I think of people—therapists included—as having lots of different parts, as well as a kind of 'core' self. Therapists can get triggered in a variety of ways. One of these parts will take over and they don't make for very good therapy. My goal when I am working is to try to maintain what I call 'self-leadership' most of the time. I have my parts around, but I won't have them taking over—especially the ones that have extreme reactions to people. It's a different take on countertransference.

"The parts of me that have gotten me in trouble would include parts that can be very impatient and think that therapy is taking too long. My client will pick up on that, and again you get protection and resistance based on the client's sense of judgment from this part of me. That starts a vicious cycle."

THE PARTS THAT GET ME IN TROUBLE

There is Dick's "impatient self" that leads him to push clients to do things before they are ready, the part that wants to be entertained even if it means that the pace will be rushed at the client's expense. We asked about other parts that may get him into trouble.

"There is a part of me—and I think it is common in men in general—that can't stand for someone to be highly dependent and demanding things. I know that doesn't make for a good quality in a therapist but I have had clients who would get into that very needy, childlike state at times. This cold part of me would take over. I might say all the right words but there would just not be any heart in them at all. That again would make my clients' needy parts just that much more needy. They might feel abandoned by me and panic even more."

Schwartz hit this point solidly, and painfully. It hurts to admit that some of our own most difficult cases, and worst examples of our work, occur when we are triggered by people viewed as dependent, clingy, and overly needy. Of course, so many of the people we see are clients to begin with because this is their presenting style: they feel helpless and lost. They want us to tell them what to do. And we have a secret voice in our heads that screams: "Get up off your butt and do something instead of whining so damn much!"

We thought this, but didn't say it out loud. We asked Dick to supply an example of a failure that he was willing to talk about.

"The worst?" Schwartz asked.

"Yeah," we prompted him. "The worst you've ever had."

"I don't think I will talk about my worst."

"Okay then," we said, "your second worst."

"My second worst?"

"All right. All right. How about one in your top five?"

Negotiations out of the way, Schwartz began his story.

I WASN'T PREPARED

The case selected occurred a number of years ago. We noticed that this was a common theme among the people we interviewed. It was as if it was still too raw and painful to talk about the failures that had occurred most recently.

"This was early in my career, working with survivors of abuse. I wasn't prepared really. I kind of got into this work without much supervision and in kind of a blind way. I wasn't prepared for all the dramatic shifts that people will go through.

"There was one client, in particular. She would become very needy at times and this would trigger the cold part of me that I mentioned earlier. This would make her even more needy and demanding. At some point when I wasn't budging, another rageful part of her would come in and that would trigger this very critical part of me. I would start to see her in a very negative light. In my head, I think of her as being highly manipulative and tapping a part of me that was scared of her. When I got that kind of negative cast, and started to dread having sessions and hoping she wouldn't show up, that leaked out. You can't really hide that, although I would try to."

Once his negative feelings leaked out, the client would sense his critical judgment and feel even more worthless. Schwartz pointed out that, typical of many abuse survivors, the worthlessness would be further fueled by his own reactions. "She needed to prove that it was me who was wrong. She would be even more verbal on different aspects of what I was doing and how I was handling the therapy and what I was wearing that day. So things started to escalate."

LOOKING FOR WAYS TO UNLOAD

We asked Schwartz what it was about this case that made it bad therapy. We had several hypotheses in mind but wondered what he identified as most significant. His answer was not what we expected.

"The fact that I didn't get consultation is what made it ultimately bad therapy. When parts of you take over, as was true for me, you don't even know that you are out of line. Therapists are good at justifying everything they are doing and saying and feeling and putting it all on the client. We say what a crazy client she is and how much trouble she is. So you feel more and more saddled with her and you start looking for ways to unload her on somebody else or a hospital or something like that."

"Is that what you did in this case?"

"Yes. That is ultimately what happened. She was hospitalized. And I was relieved. And someone else took over the treatment."

"So in one sense, you were let off the hook, but on the other hand, you are still haunted by this particular case so you didn't let yourself off the hook."

"Exactly," Dick agreed. "As I got more experience I realized my own role in things. I felt righteous until I saw how much differently I could have handled things. It does still haunt me."

WORKING WITH THE PARTS

We asked what Schwartz learned from this case. He said that it wasn't so much this one failure that got his attention but rather it was a continual state of evolution for him to notice the parts of him that got in the way of doing his best work.

"I really have had to force myself to find those parts of me and work with them, talk to them, listen to their stories about why they feel the need to jump in at certain points. I need to trust in me more and let myself keep my heart open, even in the face of the rage, dependency, the neediness, or whatever parts of my clients that are coming at me."

So, what was the message in this for others?

"Do your own work. Meaning really notice countertransference, or the various thoughts or protective behaviors that get triggered by clients. Instead of keeping the focus on the clients, we should go inside ourselves and see what we can do to come back. Many therapists don't even notice this. They are totally oblivious when their stuff is going on."

Schwartz had a number of suggestions related to this issue. He urged therapists to become more aware of their internal thoughts and feelings, their various parts, as they are working. He asked clinicians to monitor very carefully what might be getting in the way. Most of all, he believed it was important that we not put all the focus—and the blame—on clients when things are going poorly. Instead of looking at the client's nasty behavior we should be looking more at our own role in causing it.

Certainly one of the things that therapists are inclined to do when we get in trouble is to blame the client as resistant or difficult. Second, as Schwartz pointed out, we like to label them with some nasty names like *borderline* or *narcissistic* or *hysterical.*

"I am not radically against diagnostic labels. What I am against is all the connotations that they bring to therapists and all the presumptions that people make when they hear them. It is frequently a waste of time spending all that energy trying to figure out which label is the right one."

SOME ADVICE

We asked Dick what other advice he had for others to avoid the pitfalls that lead to probable failure. He distinguished what might be helpful to beginners versus more experienced practitioners.

"Often, for good reason, beginners feel very insecure about what to do. Clients will sense that lack of confidence. When they get the sense that the therapist is nervous, then they are going to be much more resistant, and rightly so in some cases. Their resistance then scares the therapist just that much more.

"When I am working with beginning therapists I try to help them with those very anxious parts that make them either push too hard or become totally passive and let clients do whatever they want. A lot of beginning therapists get impatient with themselves."

Schwartz mentioned how this pressure to produce quick results was the result of the whole brief therapy and managed care movements during the 1990s. "There is a kind of built-in urgency to the work that I think also gets in the way. As soon as clients sense that you are in a hurry, and you don't think that things are moving as fast as they should, again you get these vicious cycles going." So, the whole climate of our jobs lends itself to pushing things as fast as we dare.

"When I run training programs I am helping people unload an awful lot of things they come with. A lot of beliefs. Beliefs about hiding yourself behind professionalism would be another one. You shouldn't let clients know how much you care about them or you shouldn't give them hope for fear of giving them false hope."

Among the myths that Schwartz mentioned, he said that we are trained to be as opaque as possible. If a client wants to know how we feel about them, instead of answering, we ask them why they want to know that. "A lot of that just drives these approval-needing parts of clients crazy. And for no good purpose really."

MAKING APOLOGIES

When people learn to do therapy, beginners have expectations that they will do it perfectly. When things don't go as smoothly as expected, panic can set in. The last thing that a therapist would do is acknowledge a mistake, much less apologize for it. But we happened to know that this was exactly what Dick was prone to do. From having watched him work before, we had frequently seen him apologize to clients.

"My experience is that clients really appreciate it. They feel like their perceptions are finally validated. Here is somebody who is not going to try and pretend they are right and the client is wrong, which is what their family usually did."

It was almost as if Schwartz used the apologies as a strategy to take a one-down position and empower his clients, to make them the ones in charge. He disagreed, saying it was just a way for him to be himself.

HANDLING RESISTANCE

Schwartz remarked that there were a lot of very bad ideas in our field about what resistance is and what it means. "From my point of view, when clients resist it's their right to do so, and sometimes the duty of these protective parts of them to slow down the pace and make sure you know what you are doing. The goal is to not let you go into territory they are not ready to go into. It's best to go into any client system, whether it is an individual or family or couple, with that kind of respect for the system's protectors. Instead of trying to push past them, listen to the fears they have about letting you do what you think you need to do. Then you find you have less resistance."

It struck us that Schwartz was willing to assume a lot of responsibility for the outcomes of his work, both successful and not so successful, rather than blaming the client as resistant or unresponsive. We considered that some clinicians may first blame their clients when things go wrong. If that doesn't work, the next excuse will be to blame the model they are using: perhaps it is too limited or too rigid or too something. But Dick favored the far riskier position of being himself, and then looking at himself when things didn't work out well.

"The kind of therapy that I am inviting is a riskier kind of therapy for your ego because you get more involved. It does take more of an investment on the part of the therapist and you do kind of eliminate all those different protective barriers—not all of them, but the common protective barriers we have for keeping a kind of distance."

We noticed that our participants were on a continuum. Some were at one end of this line, where they see that failure (or success) belongs primarily to the client; he or she is the one who does the work, and also the one who lives with the consequences. If the client isn't sufficiently motivated, or focused, then nothing the therapist can do will help very much. Yet on the other end of the continuum were those like Schwartz who saw the results of their work clearly related to their own skills and efforts. There was little attempt to diffuse responsibility for the outcome.

"I think you get the sense from my earlier comments that it is my belief that if I can hold that self-leadership place that I have been describing then I won't have many failures. When I have failures it is generally because I didn't hold that. *Success* and *failure* aren't perhaps the best terms for it either, because there are a lot of outcome criteria that don't necessarily capture what happens, and some of the goals that I have might be counter to some of the more traditional goals of outcome measures. When I have been able to make a self-to-self connection with someone and have been able to respectfully handle their protective parts and get to some of their very wounded parts, we generally don't fail."

Chapter 7

WILLIAM GLASSER
I Can't Wait Until You Leave

WILLIAM GLASSER is one of the most influential theoreticians in the history of counseling and psychotherapy. The creator of reality therapy, he has revolutionized the field of therapy with his classic, influential works: *Positive Addiction, Reality Therapy, Choice Theory,* and *Reality Therapy in Action.* Glasser has remained a vigorous advocate of school reform well into his 70s. His books on education, including *Schools Without Failure, The Quality School, Choice Theory in the Classroom,* and *The Quality School Teacher* apply his theory of learning to those environments where he believes children need the most help. More recently, Glasser has turned his attention to chronic health problems such as in his book *Fibromyalgia: Hope From a Completely New Perspective.*

Although it has been over 15 years since Glasser has practiced therapy, except in demonstrations on stage during workshops and lectures, he has still spent considerable time thinking and writing on the subject. His latest books, *What Is This Thing Called Love?, Getting Together and Staying Together,* and *Every Student Can Succeed* continue to advance his mission to develop internally controlled methods for improving personal effectiveness.

LOOKING BACK

Trying to be as helpful as he could, Bill Glasser began with an apology. "The truth," he admitted, "is that I can't think of any horrible mistakes I've made. I probably made them but I've blotted them out."

"Denial is a wonderful thing," Jeffrey prodded him.

"Oh, especially for me. I'm a great denier. Memories of bad things leave me almost instantly."

Actually, Glasser has a remarkable memory, going back over the 50 years of his career as a psychiatrist. The truth of the matter is that the whole subject of failure is an enigma to him. Failure represents giving up and he has devoted considerable effort to banishing that word from his vocabulary and thinking. He even titled one of his books *Schools Without Failure* to emphasize how important it was to focus on behavior and consequences rather than negative evaluations of performance.

Looking back on his own half-century career, Glasser recalled two patients he worked with who committed suicide, but in both cases he couldn't think of anything he could have, or should have, done differently.

"In one case, I was a psychiatrist at an orthopedic hospital and there was a real suicidal guy with back pain, the kind that drugs couldn't touch. I sensed that he might commit suicide so I took every precaution I could think of. I put him in a mental hospital. I wrote suicide precautions. I warned the nurses to look out for him. I didn't have many patients in there but I still talked to the nurses. I said I'm not writing this down for the fun of it; this guy is *really* suicidal. And then at 4 in the morning that same day I put him in the hospital I got a call saying he had hanged himself from the bedpost.

"And then I was sued. That was the first time I was ever sued because the hospital wouldn't cover me on their insurance and I only had $5,000 insurance. I never figured I would ever be sued but the judge dismissed the case almost instantly when he heard my story and saw my notes."

AT A LOSS

Glasser pointed out that this first example was surely a bad experience but it wasn't bad therapy. There was another case, however, that came to mind for him that was still upsetting to him. He had been seeing a woman in therapy who eventually decided to leave her husband. The man threatened that he would kill himself if she followed through on this course of action and he was most convincing in this proclamation. This was a very wealthy man who was used to getting his way. In desperation, he asked only that she agree to spend two months a year with him; that was all he wanted.

"The wife had moved to Spain but when she next visited, I didn't know what to do. I told her what the situation was and how worried I was about the guy. I said to her, if you don't give him those two months he's going to die. Now I don't know if that was the correct thing to say or what. It still haunts me."

The wife insisted there was no way she was going to give in to this blackmail. She decided that it wasn't her problem what the guy did with his life. Glasser was the psychiatrist so he could fix it.

"I just didn't know what to do, or whom to call. I mean the man was not insane. In those days, there was no chance whatsoever of getting someone committed who was reasonably sane. I thought of calling the police. I didn't even know what to say to him."

Glasser did confront the man, and did try to negotiate a suicide contract, but the patient just responded by saying that it was his life and he could do what he wanted with it. Bill tried convincing the man to check himself into a hospital but the guy thought that was pretty funny. "Why," he said to Glasser, "would I want to go into a hospital? They'll only try to stop me from killing myself."

In a strange way, this logic made sense. The only thing that Glasser could think of doing at that point was to ask the wife to write a letter detailing that she had been warned about the situation and chose not to get involved. Since she felt no guilt or responsibility, and most likely felt tired of the guy's manipulations, she was more than happy to comply with the request. At the very least, this would protect him from a lawsuit.

"Then one day when he was supposed to be at my office he didn't show up. I called the house and he didn't answer. Fearing the worst, I drove about 10 miles to his home. It was locked up tighter than a drum. I banged on the doors and screamed as loud as I could. I knew he was in there so I called the police. When they broke in they found him dead."

OTHER OPTIONS

Glasser still wonders what he could have done. "Did I do something wrong? Was this bad therapy?" Ultimately, he still can't decide. Certainly, the outcome was pretty awful but the therapy itself was handled in a professional way.

When he was asked what he might have done differently, it was obvious that even after all these years Glasser was still pretty upset about what happened. Sounding more like a humanist than the man who popularized the systematic problem-solving method that has been his hallmark, the depth of Glasser's anguish still resonated.

"What I could have done—I did this with a few other people—is sat with him for a long period of time. Maybe I could have shown him how much I cared." Bill paused for a moment, then added: "In all my years of practice, this was the most disturbing thing I faced."

RECENT TIMES

Since this episode occurred a long time ago, we pressed him about a more recent experience with ineptitude.

"The way I practice," Glasser explained, "it doesn't lead me to many bad situations. I don't really probe into patient's past lives. They tell me about things and I listen. I focus on the present. I don't talk about their symptomatic problems, you know, if they are upset or miserable or anxious or tense or depressed or have anxiety attacks. But I just can't think of any recent troubles."

Again we were struck by what a good sport Glasser was being, agreeing to talk about a subject that doesn't really fit into his thinking. If it hadn't been for his close relationship with Jon, he would never have agreed. We asked him about therapy he does on stage, but he couldn't recall getting in trouble in those structured situations. What about supervision he had been doing when teaching reality therapy? He doesn't do supervision. Well then, what about mistakes when he was teaching or doing a workshop? I turned out that Glasser is pretty forgiving of himself, a lesson that we both took to heart considering how hard we are on ourselves.

We were just about to cut the conversation short when Glasser dug a little deeper and remembered one case he wanted to tell us about. But again, he wasn't sure if this was what we are looking for.

"I saw this wealthy woman from Beverly Hills, the mother of several daughters I had been seeing in therapy for some time. I don't even remember why she was coming to see me. This mother—I've never had a feeling like this with a woman before. She was one of the most obnoxious people I had ever met in my life.

"I was desperate for patients at this time in my life. I'd see people for next to nothing. I only agreed to see the mother in the first place because I didn't want to lose the daughters from my small practice at the time. Anyway, the mother must have liked what I was giving her kids because she wanted some of it too.

"I didn't like this woman at all. I remember her telling me how rich and powerful her family was. She used to say that when they needed a favor from the Governor of California he would come to *their* house. I despised her right from the start and I only saw her this one time.

"Just as the session was about to end, I made the big mistake of telling her just what I thought of her. This was not a nice person. She was not educated. She was not polite. She just happened to be married so some rich guy so she believed she was more important than anyone else, even the governor.

"I told her that I just felt uncomfortable talking to her. I didn't like the way she presented herself. I felt antagonistic toward her. Then I said to her, 'I can't wait until you leave.'"

Bill laughed heartily at his own brashness. Then to his disappointment, the woman didn't blow up or become offended by his comments. She walked out satisfied that she had proven what a low-life and incompetent professional Glasser really was to lose his cool like that. All along that had been her goal.

Glasser thought this might have been bad therapy because he didn't end up helping the mother or the daughters in the process. He let her get underneath his skin. But he learned a lot from the experience. "I tried to be more careful after that. I can't recall a time when I ever lost my cool like that again.

Even so many years later, Bill still feels a little embarrassed about his lapse. "The whole thing made me feel kind of weak as a psychiatrist. I should have handled it better, maybe the poor woman came in and really did need something and I rejected her."

DEFINING OUR TERMS

In the struggle to help Glasser settle on examples of his less than exemplary work, we decided to go back a little and get him to define for us how he defined poor work. It turned out that he did have a fairly specific idea of what this meant, a conception that was clearly part of his theoretical writings.

"To me, bad therapy takes place when the therapist sends the message to the client that, 'You are mentally ill. You can't take care of yourself without me.' This was just how I was taught when I was in my residency—that schizophrenic people are crazy and they will never be sane. I never felt that way about anybody, even the craziest people I saw. I always felt that in a short period of time they would at least talk sane to me, which they did. That doesn't mean they became sane but it told me they were choosing to be insane and not wanting to be sane."

Even after all those decades of preaching the message that people have far more choices than they think they have, Bill still became frustrated with the long-standing resistances to his ideas, especially by the medical establishment that insists on viewing emotional disorders as purely organic problems that are best treatable with drugs.

"Bad therapy," Glasser explained further, "occurs when you tell people that they need help, and that only I can fix you. You've got something wrong that you can't figure out and you need me to do it for you."

Glasser was now on a roll, talking more and more passionately about his unique ways of defining what was good and bad therapy. He remembered a time in the early 1960s when he published his first book, *Mental Health or Mental Illness?* He was preparing to pass his Board Exams in neurology and was asked to define the difference between affect and emotion as one of the questions by the examiners. Just the fact that these prominent psychiatrists and neurologists believed this was an important distinction only reinforced Glasser's belief that they didn't have a clue about what was good treatment for patients.

SHOWING MISTAKES

We asked Glasser about a phenomenon that had always bothered us. So many leaders in our field do workshops, presentations, or write books about their approaches to therapy and they almost always present cases of rather spectacular successes and almost never talk about their failures.

We hoped Bill would be willing to address the subject of making good impressions versus teaching therapy the way it really occurs behind closed doors. He easily warmed to the subject. "I've probably done as many workshops as anyone else around. First of all, I never show a demonstration video. I only do an actual demonstration with someone playing a role or playing himself."

Aha, we thought, that is one reason why he doesn't get in trouble so much, because his "clients" are playing roles. Even if they are really playing themselves in one form or another—and all role playing is still being a part of yourself—there is still less emotional activation. Another reason, as Glasser mentioned earlier, is that he stays pretty much in the present and doesn't dig up painful stuff from the past. Third, he presents a highly structured problem-solving approach.

"I really don't care at conferences what the volunteer clients do. But I don't think it's fair to show an edited video. Even in the book, *Reality Therapy In Action,* I did point out in at least one place, and maybe several places, where I think I didn't do the right thing. There's one point where I just admit I made a mistake."

This is unusual indeed. Most often, when writers include case examples in their books or articles, they include those that support their ideas rather than present conflicting data or show them in a less than favorable light. Glasser continued talking with increasing candor. "Making a mistake in therapy is so easy to do. We're all aware of this. Most often, this occurs when the client withdraws. Of course, this could easily be edited out of a video, which is why I prefer to do live demonstrations."

When pressed for other examples of mistakes he had made, Glasser linked the conversation to Maslow's "hierarchy of needs" and his own "choice theory." He pointed out that because people have a genetic need to be loved, approved of, and to belong to intimate groups, we were all inclined to avoid doing anything that pushed others away and more disposed to saying and doing things that bring people closer. Of course, this is the original template, as designed, rather than the way things turn out for many people who are exposed to situations or an environment that recalibrates these settings.

"I think having my theory all set up in my head guides what I'm going to say or do. Sometimes I think I've gone a little bit too far with this and too fast. Sometimes I'm not careful enough to build a relationship with the client before pointing out that he or she may have made some bad choices."

A SURPRISING TWIST

Bill Glasser may be known primarily for his work as a brief therapist and school interventionist, but as he has gotten older he values his relationships with people as more and more significant. He returned to the earlier case of the man who killed himself and wondered once again whether there wasn't something more he could have done to show how much he cared. Other cases came to mind, as well, in which it was the relationship he established that proved most beneficial rather than any specific technique.

"I had the one client, Larry, whom I saw on and off for 35 years. I never felt I did much with him in terms of therapy. But I stopped him from killing people. He had all these rifles that really bothered me, so I kept them in my office for four years. This was soon after the guy in the tower at the University of Texas shot all those people."

There was pride in Glasser's voice in the extent to which he had felt committed to the people he had helped. Looking back over his career, it was not his theoretical contributions or therapeutic techniques that come to mind but rather his relationships with people.

What about his weaknesses as a clinician?

Glasser admitted that he had been impatient and might push someone faster than he or she was ready to go. But because he had learned from his mistakes, he was quick to apologize once he realized what was going on, and then to move at a more appropriate pace.

WAKE UP NOW DR. GLASSER

Another reason why Glasser doesn't believe that he does bad therapy very often is because he views the client as the one in charge, the one who does all the work. "In my therapy, I always explain to people, as much as

I can, what I am doing and why I am doing it. I understand therapy pretty well since I got involved in choice theory. Like when I do a role-play before an audience I'm always desperately hoping for a really tough client, someone who will challenge me." This led to Glasser's admission that boredom had been a problem for him throughout his career. Most clients do not present him with much of a challenge.

"I've fallen asleep in sessions before," he said with a laugh. Now, surely *that* would be bad therapy we pointed out.

"Well, I talked with my supervisor about that and he told me that if clients can't keep you awake, then Goddamn it, go to sleep! "I'd have some clients I'd fall asleep on and think they'd got used to it and they would say, 'Wake up now, Dr. Glasser. I'm going to tell you something important.'"

One of the ways that Glasser remained creative and energized in his work was by pushing the limits of what he knew and could do. He trusted his intuiton and creative system to give him what he and the client needed most.

"I did a role-play the other day and I don't think I ever did anything exactly like this before. This woman was really seriously depressed. I mean she was lower than a rug on the floor. So I said to her, 'Usually when I see people, I don't believe they have such serious problems and they don't need that much help. But I have to tell you: You are about the most seriously upset, miserable, and unhappy person that I've dealt with in a very long time. And it just makes me happy that you came in to see me.' And of course the person had trouble dealing with that."

So then, was *that* bad therapy? We were a bit puzzled about where he is going. "No," Glasser explained, "not at all. I'm saying that when I feel stuck I depend on my creative system to figure out what to say or do. Sometimes it doesn't work, but that's not bad therapy."

Again we were struck by how forgiving he was of himself. One of the reasons that many practitioners are afraid to take risks in their work, or to be more creative, is that they are terrified of making a mistake.

FUTURE DIRECTIONS

Although he was at a time in his life when many people retire, Glasser was eager and excited about the new work he was doing every day. His lecture and workshop schedule might be reduced a little but his mind was always racing with new ways to apply what he knew to help others.

"I am doing therapy all the time. Like yesterday my computer printer broke down. It had been working for about 10 years and it finally died. I just called a repair guy from the phonebook. He was such a nice man.

He came in and it was like more to see me than he was fixing my machine. I made a relationship with him. We talked. I praised him about how I never expected anyone to take this thing apart and do everything and show me stuff. I said no other repairman could do this. Nobody else could do what he does. When I meet people like this, I try to make a relationship with them."

We found it interesting that as Glasser had matured and aged it appeared as if he had evolved into a form that even Carl Rogers would have approved. His warmth and essential kindness and caring seemed the key to who he was and what he did.

This discussion of relationships reminded Glasser of another project that he had been involved with. "I recently wrote a book about fibromyalgia. This is an increasingly serious problem that is afflicting more and more people. This guy that works with me picked me up with this really beautiful woman in the car. This woman had fibromyalgia. I really wanted to help her and she became angry, I mean really incensed.

"She said to me, "You can't help people like me. Nobody can help me. This is a disease that's incurable.'

"When I pointed out that she was choosing how to behave with her problems, she became even more angry. How could I dare insinuate that all the pain and misery she was suffering were the result of her own choices?"

Glasser seemed surprised that the woman was so ungrateful for his attempt to offer her what he believed was constructive help. He almost felt hurt that his help was rebuffed, even though what this person seemed to want most at the time was understanding rather than to have her problem fixed or her beliefs challenged.

Glasser shrugged, admitting, "I guess you've got to be a little careful. I didn't say it in a tough way or anything. But people really are invested in when they've got chronic pain. They are really invested in it. You imply that they have anything to do with it and boy, wow! I learned from that to be a lot more careful. Now when people buy my book I tell them that if they don't like what I say, it's okay."

Our conversation drew to a close as we continued talking about the challenges that chronic pain sufferers experience and what can be done to help them. This subject really excited Bill. It is something that he would like to devote the rest of his life to working on.

Chapter 8

STEPHEN LANKTON
Speaking the Client's Language

STEVE LANKTON was trained as a social worker and Ericksonian hypnotherapist. He lives and works in Arizona where he runs a practice specializing in family therapy, brief therapy, and corporate consulting. He is a gifted and creative clinician who has successfully combined his work with Milton Erickson and neurolinguistic programming into a pragmatic, relationship-oriented approach. Lankton is author of several books including *Practical Magic, The Answer Within, Enchantment and Intervention*, and *Tales of Enchantment*.

Our conversation took place just two days after the terrorist attacks in Washington and New York. Lankton was badly shaken by the events and uncertain if he could focus on the subject at hand. We decided to talk for awhile and see what came out. Feeling very vulnerable, he started tentatively, and then seemed to lose himself in the conversation. What emerged is a picture of a highly sensitive and reflective practitioner who had given a lot of thought to his mistakes and failures.

IN SHOCK AND THEY DON'T KNOW IT

We began by talking about how each of us was doing in response to the recent tragedy. We observed that a number of our students were experiencing a lot of posttraumatic stress but that they didn't seem to be aware of it. They see symptoms in others but not in themselves. Some of them were crying inexplicably and yet felt uneasy because they didn't know why. They felt guilty because they didn't really know anybody who was hurt so they didn't feel they were responding very rationally. Each of us personalized our own reactions to the incidents and shared the ways in which we were trying to be helpful to those around us.

In this atmosphere in which failure and recriminations literally hung in the dusty, choked air of Lower Manhattan, endlessly second-guessed by the media, we launched into our questions about bad therapy. This was an interview in which we actually had to prompt our participant very little. Lankton started talking right away about what he saw as bad therapy.

LET ME TELL YOU SOMETHING, SONNY

Lankton saw bad therapy as falling into several general categories, the first of which occured when you failed to engage with the client. You ended up wasting your time with any number of fancy techniques, none of which proved useful, because of a basic failure to build a solid, collaborative relationship.

"I had a client come in for back pain," Steve said, launching into an example. "He was referred by a psychiatrist. While I was waiting for this new client, I saw this guy out the window getting out of his car. His wife was helping him with every step. I noticed an absolute lack of participation on his part in any of that help. He didn't shift his body weight; he didn't do anything voluntarily to help her. I thought to myself, 'Wow, that guy is really torturing his wife.'"

It turned out, of course, that this man was Lankton's new client. The guy slowly and painfully shuffled into the office, being helped by his wife every step of the way. What struck Steve again was how his body language signaled someone who was trying to be as uncooperative and resistant as possible. Lankton greeted the man at the door, showed him to his seat, and then asked how he could be of service.

"Well," the man said, "let me tell you something, Sonny." Being addressed in such a way did not exactly endear him to his new therapist. First of all, this man was about the same age as Lankton, and second, he responded in that tone and manner to everything that Lankton suggested.

"So," Steve tried, "have you tried self-hypnosis?" Lankton had had success in the past using this method for pain management.

"Let me tell you something, Sonny. I never tried hypnosis and I'm never gonna try hypnosis." This answer puzzled Lankton because he knew the psychiatrist referred his patient in the first place for hypnosis. He was certain the man would have been told that.

Lankton decided to try a more indirect approach. "Let me tell you a couple of stories about clients I have had who have used self-hypnosis and how it has worked for them." The plan was to inspire and motivate the man with noteworthy stories of success. Lankton related several such cases in which people with chronic pain responded well to treatment, even years after the sessions ended.

"So," Lankton asked him, "what do you think about that?"

"Let me tell you something, Sonny. I don't think it happens like that."

Taken aback, Lankton wondered if he was being called a liar.

"You can call it anything you want to."

"Okay," Lankton answered promptly, "then I'd like to just call it a day. If you ever get to thinking about this in a way that would make you want to give it a shot, then you call back." Steve stood up and walked the couple to the door. Just as they reached the waiting room, the man turned and offered Lankton his hand.

"Tell you what," Lankton told him, "I'll shake your hand next time I see you."

"Now *that* was a failure," Steve announced with a good-natured laugh that belied the embarrassment he still felt over mishandling this case.

As the man slowly limped out the door, Lankton stared at his own hand and studied his strong negative reaction to what had happened. He heard Milton Erickson's voice whispering to him in the back of his head: "You know how you could have engaged that client, Steve? You could have told him how you see some people where their wives are really a pain in the neck and sometimes the only thing you can do is stay with them and torture them. Some people are so dumb they torture them by being mean all the time. If you really want to torture them, the best way to do it is to kill them with kindness. Some people don't know how to be a gentleman and do that."

Lankton reflected that he should have done something similar to engage this man, to speak *his* language rather than insisting that the client meet him on his preferred ground. He concluded the story by explaining that this is one kind of bad therapy, the sort where he wasn't willing to invest the hard work involved in meeting the man on his terms. Steve shrugged as he said that, admitting that he was so frustrated that he found it hard to exercise the flexibility that was needed.

THE OTHER KIND OF FAILURE

If the first example illustrated failure in which nobody got hurt—just a waste of time—then the second type resulted in clear negative outcomes. Lankton considers himself fortunate (and skilled enough) that it has been relatively rare that he has hurt anyone through his mistakes or miscalculations. There is one case, however, that is still painful for him to talk about, especially during this time when he was feeling so raw and vulnerable.

"She was a young woman who had a lot of self-doubt and social anxiety. She had a number of problems that she kept to herself. She was a little bit frantic in telling her story because in her view—and this is crucial to my mistake—she had been the victim of sexual abuse in a satanic cult. She had come up with this understanding with her previous therapist who had helped her unearth this traumatic reason behind her state at the time."

Lankton stopped to explain that he thought that dissociative and multiple personality disorders were being grossly overdiagnosed. He had serious doubts about whether a number of reported involvements in satanic cults had really, in fact, occurred. This was especially true with this woman. There was something about her story that struck Lankton as false, or at the very least, distorted.

"She was extremely unwilling to provide any details of what she meant, only saying that she had dealt with the issues in her previous therapy. This made me question whether that therapy had been complete. Of course, I didn't confront her nearly as boldly as I have said it to you. I knew that if I showed any degree of doubt she would begin to mistrust me. She would put me in a category as someone who wouldn't be able to help her. I would be one of those infidels who didn't believe the truth of these things, or even part of them. She didn't appear to have a paranoid personality structure; she simply appeared to be believing this because of her previous therapy."

Steve could hear a warning in his head, this one telling him to back off. "Can't you just treat her and overlook that she's not coming to find out what the truth of the past was? She's trying to find out how she can operate without anxiety in the social world. We can probably solve that problem with her. She seems to think well and has a lot of resources."

This time, Lankton listened to the warning. Since the past may not have been critically relevant to her presenting complaint, he side-stepped the issue altogether and focused in on her social avoidance. Sure enough, over the course of the next eight weeks she made steady progress.

"She really earned my trust and I earned hers. I say it in that order, instead of the other way around, because someone who wants to steadfastly hold onto something, and not reexamine it, is always a little suspect in my mind."

Lankton clarified that he wasn't asking her to look at her past in a painful way but just look at the facts. "If you asked me if my father was really an American I don't have to start thinking I distrust you because you asked me that question. I can say, 'Well, here are the following facts that I know.' It doesn't have to be an emotional battle right there. Since she did react so emotionally, I wondered whether or not I was overlooking some other feature."

Since the issue hadn't come up in awhile, Lankton had just ignored it as well, concentrating on the business at hand. The woman was delighted with the results and Lankton considered this case a huge success. End of story. Almost.

It was at this point that Lankton should have definitely quit while he was ahead. But with perfect 20/20 hindsight, he now recognized that he made a terrible mistake. In his defense, the choice he had made to continue treatment seemed entirely reasonable, but Lankton would not let himself off the hook so easily.

The woman was feeling so good about her progress in social situations that she brought up her strong fears about sexual contact. She claimed that she had been unable to have an orgasm and she was embarrassed about bringing this up to any of her dates.

Eager to build on their newly found success, Lankton suggested that this might be an issue that they could work on together. He stopped at this point to explain what a critical mistake this was in their relationship. Because he felt so much trust with her, he felt perfectly comfortable making this transition from one problem to another, even though the sexual issue was extremely emotionally charged for her. Perhaps his wording was awkward, but Lankton said to her: "I can help you learn to have an orgasm."

When he saw the look of horror and shock on her face, he clarified what he meant. "Let me explain. You wouldn't have the orgasm in my presence or in the office. You would simply have it in the context in which it was appropriate to have it." In spite of his efforts to explain what he meant, the woman remained suspicious and started to withdraw.

Disturbed by the direction things had now taken, he tried to explain further that this sort of treatment was something he had used several times before with great success. He tried to explain the sort of sensate focus exercises that would be used, all in the privacy of her own bedroom. He mentioned the success rate for this sort of difficulty. And most of all, he tried to reassure her that he had nothing else in mind but to help her. Much to his dismay, Lankton could see that there had been an apparently irrevocable breach of trust. No matter how he tried to fix things, or make things better, the client became more and more agitated and upset. She began screaming at him as she paced the room, escalating her verbal attacks further and further.

The treatment of sexual dysfunctions was familiar ground to Lankton, an area in which he had achieved consistently good results. Yet the more he tried to explain what he meant, and what the treatment would involve, the more the client became upset.

"I can't believe I ever let you use hypnosis with me," she said. "Oh, my God. I knew this would happen."

Lankton asked her why she was getting so upset.

"You knew I was in a satanic cult," she accused him.

In truth, he had forgotten this part of her life, an easy thing to do since he hadn't actually believed this story to begin with. He sensed that she might very well have been sexually abused, but he still had his doubts about the cult participation.

"What I had felt was that my relationship with her had built such trust that I could speak to her with an ease that I should not have felt. I was truly saddened by her reactions. I even had tears in my eyes as I explained to her that I would *never* do anything to hurt her. I was so sorry that this had taken away from her other success."

Lankton urged her to think things through before coming to any conclusions. He suggested that she return again when she felt more comfortable, or if she'd rather, she could even bring a third party to make her feel safe again.

Instead, the woman went directly to the referring agent and told the professional that Lankton had been inappropriate and unethical. This person then interviewed him for the purpose of clarifying the complaint. Although it was quickly concluded that there was no evidence of misconduct, just a misunderstanding, Lankton still felt awful about the outcome.

GETTING MY INTUITION SLAPPED

As we were listening to Lankton's story, we could feel our own hearts pounding in more than sympathy. Each of us could recall similar unfortunate situations in which a well-functioning relationship ended abruptly because of some inadvertent slip or miscalculation on our parts. It may have been an inappropriate joke, or an insensitive remark, or even some action that went unrecognized, but the result was the same: the client fled with no explanation. And there was no opportunity to work through the misunderstanding.

In this case, the referring agent attempted to gather data with the client's best interests in mind. Steve found the experience difficult but entirely appropriate and useful. Here was a victim of apparent sexual trauma who was now further traumatized. In addition, Lankton was feeling (and is still feeling to some extent) a lot of sadness, loss, and pain as well.

Up until this point, Lankton had been doing a lot of trauma recovery for sexual abuse. He had been doing teaching and supervision in this area as well. But after this case blew up, he decided that he felt so incompetent that he didn't want to do this kind of work anymore.

Given Steve's obvious distress over this case, we hesitated to press further. Before we could even ask the follow up question about what he learned from all this, Lankton volunteered an explanation.

"This case illustrates one of those principles that Milton Erickson drilled into my head and that I never should have forgotten for a moment. The most important thing is to speak the client's experience and language. The fact that you build good rapport with the person doesn't mean that you can forget that basic principle. It doesn't mean that you can now speak from your own experience and language and expect them to follow. Rapport doesn't open the doors as wide as you come to think it does."

FEELING VULNERABLE

From this discussion, the title of the chapter emerged about the importance of speaking the client's language. We all found it perfect in capturing the essence of both cases.

"Come on," Steve teased us, "you're both just sucking up to me because I'm vulnerable right now. You just want me to incriminate myself." We all laughed at this, but it sparked a reminder of the place where we started.

"Speaking of vulnerable, I think this isn't the best time to be asking people to become more vulnerable and open up about their cases. We are all feeling extremely vulnerable in our country right now. I was teaching in Germany just after Chernobyl, and those people acted and sounded and seemed to feel the way I'm acting and sounding and feeling right now. They were frightened for their lives in an irrational way and it wasn't quite in their consciousness. But the thoughts that they had were all so biased by this event while they weren't even aware."

Lankton made reference to our earlier discussion about our students being upset and not understanding why, and then feeling upset because they are upset because they don't know why. He then took a deep breath and admitted that he felt much better after unloading. Of course, none of us was surprised by this unburdening process. We kidded Steve further that since he was in his weakened state, perhaps he'd be willing to disclose more about his mistakes?

Again he revisited his earlier comments about the importance of remaining engaged with clients. He quoted Carl Rogers and Robert Carkhuff and evoked a term that sounded strange in the mouth of an avowed Ericksonian hypnotherapist: *phenomenological rapport.* But what he meant is that we must always keep one foot in the client's world.

The turn in the conversation got Lankton thinking more about the uses of his intuition in his work. He recalled a case in which he was able to demonstrate such complete empathy for a client that it was as if he were inside the person. He could literally see through the person's eyes.

Lankton was more than a little proud of his empathic ability so he felt especially chastised by the case he had related earlier. He had relied so much on his intuition and yet it had failed him. "My core understanding of the world was shaken. My intution was slapped."

Chapter 9

FRANCINE SHAPIRO
I Need to Have Safeguards in Place

When we spoke to FRANCINE SHAPIRO, she was right in the middle of organizing trauma treatment efforts in the aftermath of the terrorist attacks in New York and Washington, DC, just as she had done for the tragedies in Oklahoma City, Columbine, and Bosnia. "This is what I do," she said simply. Indeed Shapiro speaks with passion and excitement about the Eye Movement Desensitization and Reprocessing (EMDR) approach she started more than a decade ago. EMDR has become one of the most dramatic (and controversial) treatment methods that has emerged in recent times for treating posttraumatic stress and other psychological disorders.

Shapiro is Founder and President Emeritus of the EMDR Humanitarian Assistance Programs and is a Senior Research Fellow at the Mental Research Institute in northern California. She is the author of the several books including *Eye Movement Desensitization and Reprocessing: Basic Principles, Protocols, and Procedures*, *EMDR: The Breakthrough Therapy For Overcoming Anxiety, Stress, and Trauma*, and *EMDR as an Integrative Psychotherapy Approach*.

FAILURE TO SCREEN

The one case that Francine Shapiro returned to most often was a situation that occurred in a demonstration for a videotape. She had been asked to see a woman with lingering symptoms after a rape. Like so many of the master therapists who participated in this study, a significant part of Shapiro's clinical work takes place in the most public arenas imaginable where every mistake or miscalculation is carefully scrutinized.

Shapiro agreed to conduct a single session with the woman after she had already been seen by three or four other master clinicians. She had been reassured that this client had been properly screened and was a good candidate for this brief intervention. The case was presented as a simple, uncomplicated rape without any premorbid issues.

"Given that there was only a 50-minute window in which to help her and also demonstrate the treatment, I just entered right in with her. After an initial conversation, I asked her what the worst part of the rape was for her. She told me that it was the memory of being pinned down. This seemed to corroborate the idea I had that this was a quite straight-forward case."

Shapiro usually goes through a rather elaborate set of screening procedures that she's developed over the years. These guided imagery techniques are designed to reassure the client that things will feel safe, to prepare the client for treatment, and to conduct an assessment about the person's readiness for what will follow.

"I entered into the procedure and started out with the image of her being pinned down. Once we began the EMDR procedures the image quickly moved from being pinned down to her remembering being burned. Then she recalled a number of more horrific experiences in the rape. After that followed the aftermath of the incident where she miscarried and lost her baby as a consequence. All of the guilt that she was feeling came to the surface."

It was at this point that Shapiro realized that this was not an uncomplicated case at all, and certainly not one suitable for what she was trying to do in the limited time constraints. She was thinking that a lot more time should have been spent building trust and safety before getting into such intensely painful areas.

"At that point all I could do was try to bring her back to center and ground her. But I hadn't done the previous preparation for this. I had not put safeguards in place."

Francine was surprised on another level since four other therapists had seen this client without these issues coming out. She had every reason to trust the screening that had been done by others but it was now clear that this had not been nearly enough.

"I needed to remember what I often say about EMDR, that it is going to bring up a lot of unresolved material that's not necessarily going to come out in other forms of therapy. And it's going to happen rapidly. For those reasons, we need to have the safeguards in place for anyone, regardless of what the indications appear to be."

A CHANGE IN PROCEDURE

We asked Shapiro how this experience changed the way she operated in the future. "For one thing, I would never do that again. I would never put myself in a situation where I was allowing someone to make an assessment of the client that I was seeing. I wouldn't put myself in a situation where I didn't have the time to do the initial preparation phases of the therapy. This confirmed the need to adhere to the procedures that I had written about for years that emphasized not making any assumptions about the cases." This incident helped Shapiro to become even firmer in her commitment to never make exceptions to her safety rules.

"This is important because of the power of the therapy itself. It can take down barriers that people might be putting up. It rapidly enters into the memory network, and it brings out other unresolved issues. That is wonderful because that's part of the processing and that's what allows for the accelerated treatment effects to occur. But it also underscores the need to have these earlier safeguards."

This incident really gave all of us cause for reflection because so much of the time we trust others' professional judgments and then have to work with the consequences. Here was a situation in which several other prominent clinicians had all worked with this client so Shapiro had even more reason to skip her usual induction procedures. Yet she found the clinical situation unraveling before her eyes.

"I was rather horrified at the situation. I was thinking how difficult it was going to be to stabilize her again. I needed to bring her back in a way that she would feel ultimately empowered, and in a way that would reinforce for her that she had the ability to put disturbances aside and come out with greater self-esteem. It wasn't going to be easy because I had to invoke the authority of the clinician and a rapid introduction of my doing the guided imagery. This was basically giving the power to me. I don't believe that without transferring the power back to her that this was going to be an ultimately rewarding experience for her."

Shapiro felt concerned that perhaps she wouldn't be able to bring the client back. Although this had never happened before, she had also never encountered this type of situation in which she felt so unprepared. It took all of her experience just to restabilize things.

FROM THE SPECIFIC TO THE GENERAL

We asked Shapiro to look back over her career at some of the areas that she had struggled with the most. As she had already discussed, it is in the nature of her work that it brings up a lot of powerful material in a relatively short period of time.

"This opens the potential for multifaceted change if it is correctly engendered. Over time, I've concentrated more on what is needed to bring the really debilitated clients to a level of truly adult health."

Shapiro reminded us that many other brief approaches concentrate primarily on symptom reduction alone. In fact, that was her main focus as well during the early years. Since that time, however, it had become clearer to her that she must help people go beyond their initial complaints to look at the larger context for their difficulties.

"My challenge over these years has been to learn more about what experiences you need to engender in the office in order to let the person have a robust growth experience, to evolve as an adult who can love, bond, feel intimacy, and contribute to society. Now EMDR is used to treat a full range of anxiety and personality disorders."

It has been frustrating to Francine that her method has been misunderstood and misrepresented. She was quick to point out that while EMDR is useful as a rapid intervention for primary trauma, she was equally interested in the kind of in-depth work that is made possible after the symptoms are brought under control.

"I want to inspire that ability to grow in clients while not taking away their power. In other words, I think it is the responsibility of every clinician to make their clients know what possibilities are available. If somebody has been walking around with intense stress, with their shoulders up above their ears, reducing the symptoms halfway is wonderful. Yet the tendency of people when they are taking antibiotics is that once the major symptoms go away, they stop taking the antibiotics. My job is to make sure that clients understand where they can go and what is possible in their lives. It's finding that balancing point where you are offering possibilities but you are engaging them to recognize they have the power to achieve them. This means trying to find ways to empower clients while allowing them to engage in the possibility of more."

Shapiro feels challenged to go one step further with clients, to help them move beyond their initial symptom alleviation to do more with their lives. "You would be using the EMDR to catalyze the learning but you are also bringing in modeling, you are bringing in group work, you are bringing in systems analysis, you are bringing in guided imagery, you are bringing everything that a clinician could bring in because you are dealing with the client as a whole person. The EMDR is woven into it as a way of potentially accelerating the effects." What this has meant for Shapiro is that she has had to work very hard to identify accurately the developmental stage that a client is currently functioning in and then to match the treatment to fit the person's needs.

FEELING RESPONSIBLE

With the continued need for brief treatments to respond to victims of terror, violence, disaster, and abuse, Shapiro is often called upon to coordinate mental health services. We asked her how she dealt with this responsibility.

"When I first developed EMDR back in 1987 there were no randomized controlled studies on any form of psychotherapy for posttraumatic stress disorder (PTSD). Yet, the study that I did in 1989 was finding very rapid effects with this treatment. When I would speak to people in the Veterans Administration Hospital who were working with clients, they would be in despair because nothing seemed to eliminate the PTSD symptoms. They felt they were just marking time."

Shapiro spoke at length about how her ideas evolved and how she has trained, directly and indirectly, over 30,000 clinicians in the methods of EMDR. But she doesn't feel personally responsible for the movement because there are hundreds of other collaborators involved in the programs that provide humanitarian assistance.

"I don't think that any of us can get complacent and say that because the clients who have gravitated to our office are doing fine then the world is fine. We have to be in a place where we are not willing to leave anybody behind. So I would say a problem that I have right now would be in trying to figure out how to deal with sociopaths.

"How do you work with those who have been severely damaged through neglect or abuse in childhood? Development did not occur that allows the feelings of empathy, connectedness, bonding, and all the rest. You end up with perpetrators who cause a massive amount of suffering. These are the ones I would like to be able to concentrate a lot of effort on, to find out what we can do to help them. I don't think it is reasonable to say that anyone is beyond the reach of help."

LEARNING EXPERIENCES

Bringing the conversation back to the subject of failures and bad therapy, we spoke with Shapiro about the importance of having a forum in which master clinicians were willing to talk more openly about their mistakes. The hope was that this would make it easier for other therapists to do so in their supervision and case conferences and in their work.

Shapiro readily agreed with this premise. "There is no way to really learn unless you recognize where you have shortcomings. However, if you make an error, you can't say it doesn't matter; it was just a learning experience, because there was another human being you have to deal with. The effects on another human being cannot be dismissed in a cavalier manner. Clearly, the first thing you have to do is to make sure that the person has not been harmed. Then I can lean back and wonder where weaknesses in my own training need to be bolstered or where I have to rethink an approach."

A new theme that emerged from this conversation was the parallel challenges of taking care of the client's needs, a person who may have been injured as a result of our neglect, misjudgments, or errors, and the potential for growth in the therapist. Shapiro made clear that her first priority was to take care of the client, to repair any damage that had taken place, and then to take the reflective path to make sense of the experience.

"In that regard, it was the recognition that a previous client had not attained true object constancy that launched my interest in combining EMDR with developmental psychology. Clients can best be served by a truly integrative approach—one that combines aspects of all major approaches, and that combines practice with research evaluation."

Just as in so many of our interviews, theorists who were originally known for their work in developing specific treatment methods are now converging in their thinking, borrowing ideas from one another, looking at commonalities in what they have discovered. Perhaps, ultimately, this flexibility and openness are the best strategies of all for preventing bad therapy.

Chapter 10

RAYMOND CORSINI
Don't Get Stuck With One Approach

To generations of counseling and therapy students, Corsini's classic text, *Current Psychotherapies*, was the major introduction to theory in the profession. Now in its sixth edition, the book is still widely popular because of the way that original theorists describe their ideas in their own words.

From the beginning of his career, Corsini has been interested in integrating diverse ideas. In his *Concise Encyclopedia of Psychology* and *The Dictionary of Psychology*, he developed comprehensive resources for practitioners. He has since concentrated his efforts on bringing together different viewpoints, comparing and contrasting approaches in *Case Studies in Psychotherapy*, *Six Therapists and One Client*, and more recently, the *Handbook of Innovative Therapy*.

Corsini studied with both Rudolf Dreikers and Carl Rogers, reflecting the diversity of his training. He also mentions in passing that J. L. Moreno, the father of psychodrama, used to take naps at his house.

MULTIPLE METHODS

Corsini had been giving thought to the subject under discussion and two cases came immediately to mind. He found that in many ways the situations were similar, even though he was following two very different approaches at the time, each the legacy of his two mentors in Rogerian and Adlerian therapy. In the first case, he tried using client-centered therapy without much success, until he switched gears and tried hypnosis. In the second case, he was using Adlerian methods unsuccessfully until he incorporated psychodrama into the treatment. This theme of flexibility will be found repeatedly in his thinking, especially with regard to times when he has encountered difficulties. In fact, these two initial treatment failures led to the development of *Current Psychotherapies* and later his handbook on innovative therapies.

"The ideal therapist knows everything," Ray explained, "knows every technique and every method available. You shouldn't be stuck with any particular method." But is that possible, we asked him. In these days when the complexities of learning any one system of therapy are so challenging, how can we possibly be expected to know *all* the options available? And for beginners who are just starting out in the field, how can they possibly be expected to know "everything"; it is struggle enough just to try and hold onto the basics.

Corsini mentioned medicine as an example to clarify his point. It isn't possible for a physician to know everything in the field, but the more knowledge that is mastered, the more treatment options one has. "In therapy, we are free to be ourselves and we are not stuck with anything, whether it's psychoanalysis or Adlerian or cognitive behavior and so on. The ideal therapist, I think, is a person who has a working knowledge of many systems."

MISTAKES IN THE PAST

It was difficult for Corsini to think of examples of bad therapy in his work. One challenge to his memory was that it had been awhile since he had been in full-time practice. Second, because he was willing to try so many different methods in his work, even when he had felt stuck, he simply moved on to a different approach until he found the right combination of things that worked. Eventually Corsini settled on a case that had occurred over 50 years ago when he was the Chief Psychologist at San Quentin Prison in California.

"I was there about a week and an inmate whose name was Ken came and said to me he was a member of an organization of inmates called "The Seekers." He wanted to know if I would talk to this group that met once a month." At first, Ray was a little intimidated by the invitation because he heard that the prior meeting had Robert Oppenheimer, the lead scientist who developed the Atomic bomb, as the speaker. He agreed to give the talk to about 200 listeners and was approached afterwards by one of the inmates.

Ken scheduled an appointment with Corsini a few weeks later. He began the session by confessing: "I am a criminal. The reason I know I am a criminal is that I have been convicted three times and this is my third time in prison. Each time I have admitted that I committed the crime. That's a fact."

"Yeah?" Corsini answered him, "So, what's the problem?"

"Well," Ken replied, "I don't feel like a criminal. I don't think like a criminal. But I have acted like a criminal and I want to know why."

This struck Ray as a very good question, but he felt at a loss how to answer him. "I just don't know what I can do for you." It turned out that Ken wanted a job working in psychology in some way. He wondered if Corsini could arrange for him to help out.

"I'm a machinist," Ken said, as if that explained both why and how he could help. They eventually settled on a schedule for arranging regular sessions to work on the man's issues. "All I knew at that time was Rogerian therapy, so I saw this fellow for about three months using this listening approach. After a while I saw him twice a week, and then three times a week. Ken was a very interesting person."

As Corsini told the story, even after over five decades, it was obvious how much he enjoyed his talks with Ken, who had an assortment of concerns. Among other things, he had a habit of living with two women at the same time.

"He would marry a woman, divorce her, marry another, and then the three of them would live together. Along the way one of his ex-wives came to see him and talked to me, really a lovely lady, and she told me that this was true."

One day, Corsini's supervisor, a psychiatrist, stopped by to check on things in the office. "Who is this guy I see here waiting for you all the time?" the psychiatrist asked him.

"Just a guy I'm seeing in therapy."

"Look," the psychiatrist scolded him, "We've got 3,000 men here to help and you can't give one person all that time."

Corsini was forced to tell Ken during the next session that the counseling would have to come to an end. The client was very disappointed but understood the situation.

"Then I had an idea," Ray said. "I had tried hypnosis only once before and this was at another prison. Unfortunately, after this first attempt to do hypnosis, the man tried to commit suicide right in my office. He got on his knees and started banging his head on the floor screaming. I tried to lift him up but he was a powerful guy and threw me back. My glasses flew off. I ran around behind him and climbed on his back to prevent him from hurting himself anymore. Finally he started crying."

We could see why Corsini would have been reluctant to try hypnosis again after an experience like that. Nevertheless, because time was so limited with this current client, he decided to use it again.

"After about an hour and half, we got the complete answer to the question of his crime. It went back to his childhood when he was about 10. When Ken went out with his uncle, who was about his age, the two boys went searching for magpie eggs. The uncle was supposed to have a physical condition that limited his exercise. Ken asked him to climb a tree in the search for eggs and then the guy fell and suffered an injury to his appendix. They decided not to say anything to Ken's mother or grandmother, who was the mother of this boy. In the middle of the night, the mother woke up Ken and said that his uncle was very bad. They drove 40 miles to the nearest hospital where the boy died."

The grandmother—who was also Ken's aunt—then accused Ken of killing her son. Ken denied this but was told to leave his home and never return. They lived on an isolated farm and Ken's father was away fighting in France during World War I. Ken was forced to live in the cellar and not see the grandmother at all. It turned out that whenever someone in Ken's family died, Ken immediately was accused of a crime.

While using nondirective therapy for many months failed to make much progress, this single session with hypnosis was a real turning point. Corsini cited this as an example of the flexibility that had served him well throughout his career.

Since Ray doesn't think very often in terms of success and failure, we struggled a bit trying to hone in on where he failed with this previous case. He doesn't feel that he made a mistake with this case, or any others that come to mind, but just that it took him awhile to discover the right treatment. He does admit, however, that if the psychiatrist hadn't forced him to abbreviate his sessions, he might still have the guy in Rogerian therapy.

LOOKING AT THE POSITIVE

We were curious about how Corsini looked back over his long and distinguished career. We wondered what he saw as his greatest mistakes and weaknesses. The question didn't really trigger anything for him.

"I can't think of any weaknesses of that sort. I operated like most good therapists, with confidence that I was capable of doing anything anybody else could do. I had plenty of self-confidence and I didn't feel I had any weaknesses at all."

We asked him further what he meant by this since we were each able to articulate several areas of weakness we had struggled with in our careers. When we brought these points to Corsini, telling him how different our own experiences had been with identified weakness, it triggered further elaboration.

"At one point in my life I worked at an alcoholism clinic for about 2 years. I remember telling people that in these 2 years I had only two cases of success. People said that maybe I wasn't a good therapist, but I said that I at least had two cases, which is more than anybody else I knew who worked with this population. Still, I don't think I have any weaknesses at all that I can think of."

Ray hesitated for a moment, running over a list of possibilities. As we said, thinking in the particular way our questions led is not part of his ordinary reflective time. "I do recall that I was very careful in sexual matters not to bring them up. I think of one case that I had. This woman had been sexually abused and I wanted to find out what had happened but I didn't have the courage at the time. This was a personal failing not having enough courage to discuss it."

We talk a bit longer about the meaning of this response and noticed that Corsini used different language from our own to describe outcomes and reflect on his own performance. "I may be self-proctective but I feel everything I did worked out as well as could be expected. I didn't have any more successes or failures than anybody else. I constantly asked myself if I was as capable as I could be. I didn't know if I was a good therapist, or an average therapist, or a bad therapist. I didn't have any criteria that I could measure myself against."

It was Corsini's way not to dwell on the mistakes, especially since they were often rectified through further work. He gave us another example of what started out to be a failure, but like the other cases he recalled, this one also ended on a positive note. He had been using Adlerian therapy with a client and was not making much progress. Since at the time Corsini had become friends with J. L. Moreno, he felt encouraged to experiment with psychodrama. This pattern became the hallmark of his practice both as a clinician and as a writer.

SWITCHING GEARS

"As I think I have already mentioned, the more you know about psychotherapy the more likely you are to be good at it. Learn all these systems, all of them, and try to learn as many as possible because all have something to offer."

From Corsini's perspective, he doesn't do bad therapy, or make mistakes. Rather, when things "go bad," he just uses that data to make adjustments and switch gears. He feels bad for practitioners (and their clients) who are stuck using only one model: when things don't go well for them, they have few options about where to go next.

Chapter 11

JOHN GRAY
Being in Bad Therapy

JOHN GRAY is certainly one of the best-known writers about relationships. His book, *Men Are From Mars, Women Are From Venus*, has been one of the all-time bestsellers, spawning a dozen sequels, radio and television shows, and even a Las Vegas production. Nobody has been more instrumental in teaching the public about gender differences in communication styles.

Originally trained as a family therapist, Gray branched out into popular writing because he felt increasingly frustrated with the prevailing treatments at the time that emphasized expressing feelings at the expense of mutual understanding between partners. His original book was followed by a string of others, each one applying his observations to specific aspects of relationships: *Mars and Venus in the Bedroom, Mars and Venus Together Forever, Mars and Venus on a Date, Mars and Venus Starting Over*, and several others.

SOME BAD EXPERIENCES

It took us a bit of time to settle on the topic of conversation: Gray had thought that what we were interested in were his experiences as a client in therapy, most of which had been less than satisfactory. Grateful that he was willing to be open about the subject from the other side, we quickly switched gears and urged him to begin.

John Gray had been in marriage counseling several times in his life, all for reasons to help his wife and himself to sort out some challenges in their relationship. He had generally found it helpful when the therapist listened well and asked appropriate questions. But what really pushed his buttons were those clinicians who had been unduly intrusive. He also had serious reservations about times when the therapist would notice the slightest hint of emotion in the conversation and then probe the feelings as if he or she had hit a goldmine.

"Well John," the therapist would say, "that seems to irritate and annoy you. Let's talk about that."

"No," Gray would reply, "I think I had better just listen to what my wife has to say. After all, that's what she asked me to do." Gray's wife nodded her head in agreement. Gray would listen for awhile and then the therapist would ask him what he was feeling.

"I don't think that what I'm feeling is going to help matters much," Gray answered in irritation. "I'm feeling annoyed. And if you want the truth then what I feel is that my wife is exaggerating, overreacting, and reporting things not necessarily the way I think they happened."

"See," Gray's wife said, "he doesn't listen."

It was sessions like this that only made things worse. John commented that his therapists seemed to love probing feelings wherever they might lead. The therapist would keep pushing him to express himself, and then after he would do so, his wife would become more upset and their communication more impaired. All of this just seemed to reinforce the idea that this couple would never make it together and that they would never understand one another. Therapy only made the relationship more problematic.

Gray told the story using dialogue, as if the scene was presenting itself before our eyes.

"So John," the therapist continued, "your wife has strong feelings. Of course this is going to be unsettling, annoying, and irritating because what you want is someone who is loving and supportive and who seems to see the world the way you do. And when someone doesn't see the world the way you do, naturally you are going to get angry or feel reactive like this. The most important thing is to contain these feelings inside until she is done, until she is finished, and then take some time to look at how you feel.

"And Bonnie," the therapist continued, "you should take some time to appreciate John for listening."

Gray's own frustration and anger came flooding back as he remembered the way they were treated. "Once you are more balanced you can talk about your issues. But it doesn't serve any purpose to go back and forth, venting, accusing, misinterpreting, and correcting, and so forth. All we were doing was an exaggerated form of what was going on at home."

It was clear that Gray's own ideas about what was good for couples began to germinate while he recovered from his own bad therapy. "Here I was, the client, recognizing that this type of cure was only fueling the problem."

One of the things that has made Gray such an effective speaker and writer is his willingness to use his own life experiences, both good and bad, to illustrate his points. In this case, it was obvious how his own personal therapy shaped his ideas about how to practice it himself. This fits perfectly with our own experiences in which we learned more sitting in the client's chair than we ever did in graduate school. At the risk of probing old wounds, and being accused of doing exactly what Gray was complaining about, we prompted him to recall other experiences as a client in bad therapy.

"Going back 20 years ago, I remember bad therapy was expressing feelings and using anger therapy to pound out your feelings and really get things out. Then you were supposed to feel better afterwards. And often you did feel better afterwards but there was never any resolution that occurred. So instead of resolving a situation, just venting became the mode of operation."

Once he began doing marital work himself, Gray noticed that he would sometimes see the casualties of other therapists, mostly practitioners who were doing some forms of expressive therapy. These people could express sadness and cry on a dime, express fear and terror fluently, but they could do nothing about finding forgiveness or personal responsibility for their behavior. "The act of venting feelings could be as addictive as taking drugs.

"If you do it in the right measure it is very good. One of my favorite therapy tools is having people write out what they are angry about, what they are sad about, and what they are afraid of. I do this to clearly define what it is that is upsetting them, what it is that they are wanting and needing, and then to help them to find forgiveness."

STICKING TO FORMULAE

Gray continued, presenting his model of intervention with couples, straying a bit from the realm of his personal experiences about which he had been so honest earlier. With prompting, he was again willing to talk about a time when his usual foolproof technique failed him. Sometimes, Gray noticed that the letters would only make couples fight harder, evoking anger and resentment that could not be worked with very effectively.

As with so many of the other mistakes he had made in his career, observing the limitations of his method helped him to refine the technique. "I later recommended that people write the letters privately as a process of inner exploration and not share them with their partners. Some people really don't want to hear these sorts of things or they feel punished by them. Other people can hear the feelings and want to hear them and that is most effective."

Gray described a time when he was with one couple in which one of the partners clearly struggled with hearing the other's letter. After this episode he resolved to change the way he operated in the future. Gray remembered with regret other cases he used to work with when he was still practicing a more evocative style that encouraged couples to vent as much as possible.

The truth is that when any of us think back to the way we used to practice 20, 10, or even 5 years ago, there may be some embarrassment about our "primitive" methods that we have since outgrown or developed much further. In one sense, this work was not truly bad therapy, since we were doing the best we could at the time, using the best available practices at the time. A surgeon, for instance, would hardly become critical of doing cardiac bypass operations 20 years ago when similar symptoms can now be treated with medication.

Nevertheless, John still felt considerable regret over using therapeutic approaches that he now considered obsolete, if not downright dangerous. This brought up his awareness of other formulas that are relied upon by therapists, standard procedures that are not adjusted to the situations or client needs. We all agreed that this could indeed lead to some very bad therapy.

PUBLIC CONFESSION AFTER PERSONAL RESOLUTION

Gray talked at great length about the mistakes that he believed therapists made many years ago. When we attempted to turn the discussion back to his own personal failings, he offered a very interesting perspective on the subject.

"First of all," John explained, "my experience counseling others has been one of tremendous success and only positive experiences. The only problem that used to happen—and I don't allow it to happen now because I only do brief therapy—is that people come in with a crisis and I would help them to resolve things very quickly. Then, after we were done they just wanted to keep coming in to meet with me because they so enjoyed the experience."

We attempted to press him further about any current struggles or more recent failures. Surely there must have been a time not too long ago in which he had made a miscalculation or bungled things. We also found our own experiences to be somewhat at odds with Gray's in that "good" therapists do not always have constant successes.

"We just wondered if something stood out fairly recently when you were doing a presentation or doing a lecture where you did something that you wish you hadn't done. What did you learn from this mistake?"

That hit home immediately. "I used to let people ask questions and I don't let people do that anymore. I gave a talk to some 700 therapists in San Francisco. I was talking about Mars and Venus ideas and this woman in the back felt she had the right to stand up and start challenging me and questioning me. I said, 'Excuse me, this is not the time for questions and answers. Please sit down.'"

When the woman persisted in asking her question, Gray repeatedly reminded her that this wasn't the time to do so, politely but firmly asking her to be seated. When she still refused, he asked to her leave.

"What was going on inside you when this was happening?"

"Well, I was completely offended and shaken, like someone was attacking me. Now that I think about it, someone *was* attacking me. So here was someone who had her own political agenda, wanting to talk at one of my talks, and I won't allow it."

In his younger years Gray might very well have handled this situation very differently, and much less effectively in his opinion. We were confused, though, by this story that seemed to be another example of a success rather than a failure. We asked him once again about an example of bad therapy or bad teaching that occurred more recently.

"What is an area of weakness or some issue you are working to improve right now?"

"Nothing comes to mind," Gray insisted. "I will tell you this, though, if something *did* come to mind I probably wouldn't tell you anyway."

Now this was an interesting turn to the conversation so we probed further to find out what he meant. After all, we tried to be very clear about what we were investigating in this project—examples of bad work that resulted in significant learning experiences.

"Part of what I have learned," Gray explained, "and this is part of bad therapy to me, is that when I present I am completely open and authentic about my life regarding the issues that I have resolved. I feel that it would be irresponsible of me to propose something that I was in the middle of processing to an audience. If I'm in the middle of processing something I am in somewhat of a state of confusion and the last thing I want to do is present my state of confusion to the audience."

So Gray had a policy of using self-disclosure very carefully and strategically, restricting his personal stories only to those issues that he had fully resolved. He found it unprofessional and inappropriate to discuss anything of a personal nature about which he was currently struggling.

"If I hadn't yet processed the problem, it would be of no value to share it with an audience because I don't have the punch line. The punch line is what did I learn from it, how did I benefit from it?"

I'VE BEEN THERE AND DONE THAT

Gray tried to be as honest and open as he could during his presentations, but he was only willing to talk about problems that he had successfully confronted. He mentioned as one example how he teaches men the importance of giving flowers to women because he doesn't believe that very many of them think of it on their own. Then he told the story of how he used to forget to do this himself but had now made it part of his usual way of expressing love.

John took exception to the Freudian approach where self-disclosure of any kind is not tolerated. He believes that a therapist's personal stories can be useful, but only when they are about resolved issues. There was a bit of tension in the conversation because Jeffrey had been the one pushing John on this point. It only occurred to Jeffrey later that since he had made a whole career of talking about his unresolved issues related to fears of failure, that he and Gray had very different ideas about the value of such struggles.

"It doesn't serve a person to come into therapy," Gray said, "and he says he is depressed, and then I say I am really depressed too. I don't know what to do about it. Maybe we should both take some Prozac. That would not be helpful at all."

Yet the other kind of disclosures, those in which the therapist demonstrates that he or she has already resolved the problem that is confronting the client, these can be quite powerful.

"For example, I am not a good counselor for alcoholics because I have never been an alcoholic. I don't have it in me. But I'm a great counselor for relationships because I've had relationship issues. I'm a great counselor for anxiety because I used to have anxiety. You are a much better guide if you have been there and you got through."

Chapter 12

FRANK PITTMAN
I Take a Lot of Risks

With his soft-spoken Southern accent, FRANK PITTMAN sounds more like a poet than one of the most provocative therapists operating today. He thinks he looks like Elmer Fudd, neither particularly distinguished nor frightening. "I don't scare people much when they see me," Pittman says. It doesn't take long after he opens his mouth, however, for his clients and audiences to discover that he sees part of his job as being able to "piss people off."

Frank Pittman is a psychiatrist in Atlanta and is also on the faculty of Georgia State University. He has been practicing family therapy, working especially with couples in crisis, just about as long as anybody else alive. He's treated more families than anyone else he knows, and has probably done more bad therapy too. That's because he is willing to take the most challenging routes to helping people, pathways that are fraught with obstacles and risks.

In his bimonthly columns in *Psychology Today* and *Psychotherapy Networker*, as well as writings in such books as *Turning Points: Treating Families in Transition and Crisis*, *Man Enough: Fathers, Sons, and the Search for Masculinity*, *Grow Up: How Taking Responsibility Can Make You a Happy Adult*, and *Private Lies: Infidelity and the Betrayal of Intimacy*, Pittman's big theme is about taking responsibility for one's moral and behavioral choices and their interpersonal consequences.

SO MUCH BAD THERAPY, SO LITTLE TIME

In our conversation with him, Frank began by admitting that the question we asked him about his worst session was one of the most challeng-

ing he had ever been asked. "I do so much bad therapy it's hard to remember just one session that stands out."

Pressed to select a sample that had made the most enduring impression, Pittman found himself thinking about a case from a long time ago.
"On the other hand, there have been two in the last few weeks that have
been almost equally bad. Maybe three when I stop to think about it."

Given some of the resistance we had experienced in trying to get
some of our other contributors to admit their mistakes, we were stunned
by Pittman's openness and honesty. But given his reputation, perhaps we
should have known better.

One of his worst examples of therapy took place in the early 1970s
in front of a very large audience. "This was a family in which a young
man, who was recently out of the hospital for some reason, had moved in
with his grandmother, his mother, his aunt, and his sisters. They were all
conspiring to take care of him and to keep him from having to function
in any way. They went through a whole lot of therapists trying to find
someone who could overcome the collective impact of all of these nurturing women who wanted to take care of a useless kid."

Pittman now found himself facing this family in front of an eager
audience that was looking for him to work some magic cure. Rubbing his
hands together, he was determined to deliver what he could.

"This young man would cry and talk about how bad he felt but
didn't mention feeling bad about anything he had done or had not done.
This was just feeling bad in the way that people who have had too much
therapy feel bad. They somehow resent the fact that the whole world is
not centering around their pain and so they increase the existential pain
over all the things the rest of us are too busy to think about. About an
hour into the interview I started laughing at him."

We began laughing ourselves, not because we thought the situation
hilarious but because we recognized that this was exactly the kind of
situation that would set Pittman off: someone being irresponsible and
refusing to take charge of his life, preferring to blame others for his mis-
fortune. We asked Pittman if he thought this laughter was part of some
planned intervention.

"I don't know if it was therapeutic or not but I had to do something.
This group had paid me to come up there and put on a show. This was
back in the days of Virginia Satir and Carl Whitaker and people who
could *really* put on a show. I was just a young kid who didn't have the
power to put on a big show so I did what I could to call attention to
myself in the process of listening to this pathetic loser while his family
gathered around and patted him on the knee and said 'Poor sweet baby.'"

Pittman noticed that the more heated the session became, the more
nurturing the women became, which is just what he would have expected.

Unfortunately, what he was trying to do was to get them to back off and tell the man that he was perfectly capable of taking care of himself. And he could certainly get out of the house and find a job.

"I pointed out to him that most of the people I knew who washed dishes for a living were schizophrenic; they could wash dishes no matter how much they were hallucinating. I said that if he was really as suicidal as he claimed, there were still all sorts of dangerous jobs that he could be doing that might meet his need for self-destruction."

This was about the time that Pittman started to laugh. And the man started to cry. Pittman next asked the family what they thought the best way might be to respond to the man when he started to act so pitiful as he tried to get control of them like this. What Pittman was hoping for was an answer that involved letting him work things out on his own, but as they always had, they showed that they wanted to rescue him, even as they agreed that he could do more for himself. The man responded by complaining how mean everyone was to him.

"If I were you," Pittman said to him in a deceptively soft voice, "and I was unappreciated this much, I think I would leave home and go find people who would not complain so much about taking care of me while I sit around and don't do crap. Show them you don't need them."

Much to the surprise of everyone—including Pittman, even though he tried to act as if this was all part of a plan—the man got up, walked off the stage, and out of the building.

"I don't know where he went and I never saw him again."

The audience became very uneasy. The family started to get up and follow their wayward son, when Pittman strongly urged them to remain where they were. "I suggested to the family that they not follow him. I told them that this was an indication of what good therapy we were doing. I said that what we had been trying to get him to do was to stop collapsing dependently upon them and to get up and go do something. I tried my damnedest to get them to see this, and get the audience to see this. I told them that this was a *very* therapeutic move, one that I had fully anticipated. This was exactly what I was trying to bring about and that it was a great step toward health."

The six women looked at Pittman as if he was crazy. For a moment, he feared for his life, wondering if there might be a riot, that the audience would rise up in indignation. We kidded him that he has had lots of practice with this sort of thing before.

"I *have* had practice with that before," Frank answered seriously. Because anytime you do something therapeutic you risk making people mad at you. You are shaking them from their usual pattern and you are making them aware of the fact that they have more power than they thought they had. You are telling them that they can do things that they had not been doing before. Empowerment can be terrifying. Naturally, when you scare people this much, you have to expect a certain amount of anger toward you for this."

MAKING INVALID ASSUMPTIONS

Frank Pittman readily acknowledges that he made a terrible mistake with this awful example of his work. "The boy and his family may have benefited but my hosts did not. They never invited me back. In fact, I don't think they even took me out for dinner that night."

Pittman said that throughout his career he had made this type of mistake a lot in which he believed clients really did want to change. "You have to avoid making the assumption that these people have already figured out that what they are doing doesn't work and they are asking you to correct the error of their ways."

This point led into Pittman's ideas about what constituted bad therapy, which he saw as the kind that increases people's emotional intensity and expressiveness without increasing their sense of power. He was also quick to point out that good therapy doesn't necessarily give clients a right answer or a particular course of action that might be desirable.

"Whether they use it right away or not," Pittman said, "depends in part upon whether they think you really care about them. I used to try to ignore that as a factor. I used to try ignoring the relationship as being a major factor in therapy because it creates more bad therapy."

We were puzzled by this statement because it seemed at odds with what Pittman had just explained, that he found a caring relationship to be so critical. Expecting a provocative elaboration, we were not disappointed.

"A good therapeutic relationship creates more bad therapy than anything else a therapist can do. It gets people dependent upon the therapist. It gets people thinking of themselves as lacking some sort of power that the therapist has. In order to do therapy right, you have got to make the people you are working with feel very comfortable with you."

That was the mistake that Pittman made in the case just described. He was playing for the audience rather than addressing the needs of the family. That is one reason he doesn't like doing live demonstrations, because there is an intrinsic conflict of interest between the needs of the client and those of the therapist—which is to show off.

"If you are doing therapy right, it's not very showy. It's very warm, it is very comforting, yet at the same time it is quite confrontive. You put new information into the system but it does not make a spectacular show and it doesn't wow a crowd. When you try to make it a great show, you run the risk of alienating the people you are trying to help."

RESPONSIBLE RESISTANCE

When Frank began the conversation, he said that he did so much bad therapy he had a hard time settling on only one representative case. Thinking he was saying this in jest, we asked him what he meant by that.

"I wasn't kidding. I take a lot of risks. I'm not afraid I'll hurt people. I don't think that people are going to react to me so horribly that they are going to race out and commit suicide, splattering themselves against my building just to get back at me. I don't assume I have that much power to piss people off. Therefore, I assume that people are with me when they may not be there yet. I'm so comfortable with people I assume people are comfortable with me. I'm accustomed to being able to work with just about anybody and have that person feel good about the relationship with me. I may assume we are at that point too early in the process and I may start pointing out to people the error of their ways before they have gotten over the expectable initial resistance to me. It's natural and to be expected that they'll push me away at first and I'll back off from the point, but not from the relationship."

Pittman talked about the source of the resistance that he encounters and what that means. He finally concluded that a lot of the time he won't understand from where the reluctance stems. This reminded him of another example of bad therapy.

"I had a horrible interview not long ago with a couple. The man had gotten into an affair and had decided to leave his wife, but he wanted her to tell everybody that the divorce was her fault because he didn't want anybody to be critical of his rather delicate mistress."

We just knew that this would surely have struck a chord with Pittman and again we were not disappointed. "I thought this was a bit outrageous," he said wryly. "I thought he was expecting a bit much."

"I couldn't stop him from leaving the marriage and neither could his wife. Nor was she willing to give his mistress's delicate sensibilities a higher priority than her own needs for support from the community. I didn't even get around to telling him that if he had been as considerate of his wife as he expected her to be of his mistress, his marriage might have been quite different. I merely pointed out that his expectations of his wife's continuing loyalty, to him and to the mistress, was outrageous."

The husband became increasing angry with Pittman, perceiving (accurately) that he was being told that the marriage ending was his fault.

"You are the one who took the action that broke this marriage,"

Pittman told the husband. "And if you are going to do this, then own it. Rise up on your hind legs and act like a man. Take responsibility for it rather than acting like a wimp and blaming your wife. Needless to say, he went nuts."

Again Pittman made some assumptions that were not valid. First of all, he believed that in those first 15 minutes he had enough of a therapeutic alliance to be direct and confrontive. Second, as is so often the case when failures occur, there were things going on behind the scenes that compromised the therapy.

"I didn't know that this guy was seeing another therapist, a very well-known therapist, who just absolutely hated my book *Private Lies*. He believed that the notion that people are responsible for what they do was just an appallingly unsystemic notion. His own view was that therapy is about making sure that people's guilt is relieved. He was upset that this guy was coming to see me for couples therapy so he warned him before the interview. "'Watch out for Frank Pittman,' the therapist might have told him. 'Frank Pittman likes to make people feel guilty. He is a very mean person who wants to make you feel bad. Protect yourself from letting him make you feel bad and then come back and I will comfort you.'"

"I don't know if that was the exact message," Frank said, "but that was probably somewhat close. I didn't know what the forces were that were lined up against my effort to get this guy to take some responsibility. My view of therapy may be different from a lot of other people's. They might be good people, people who will go to Heaven. They may be wonderfully loving therapists who strongly believe that their function is to adopt people, raise them, and keep them from ever having to do anything that is uncomfortable for them or runs contrary to their feelings. But that is exactly the opposite of what I am doing."

ACKNOWLEDGING AND ACCEPTING RESPONSIBILITY FOR OUR MISTAKES

Given his openness about the subject of failures, we wondered what Pittman thought about his colleagues who were so reluctant to acknowledge their mistakes much less accept responsibility for them.

"Oh, I think a lot of us therapists are absolutely full of crap. We've taken on an extraordinary difficult job. We are operating in an atmosphere of intense pain with people who are in horrible anguish. If we start seeing things the way our patients see them, we'll end up feeling as bad as they do. Then we would be as paralyzed as they are. We have to be there in the midst of that pain while keeping ourselves sufficiently out of it. We have to maintain our ability to have hope, our ability to do reality testing. It's very hard work."

Although he was sympathetic to the difficult challenges that therapists face, Pittman also bemoaned the fact that therapists are often as reluctant to accept responsibility for their behavior as are their clients.

"We are trying our hardest to relieve pain. I don't think we see the errors being made as coming from us because our souls are pure and our intentions are honorable. We really do want to relieve pain but the kind of therapy that I do means that at just the right moment I inflict pain. Our jobs are to make people aware they are doing something wrong, that they can do something different."

Not one to mince words, Frank talked further about the kind of therapy that he does compared to what others might do. "In my usual arrogance, I see what I'm doing as surgery and what some of the other therapists are doing as massage. They are trying to make people feel better; I'm trying to really bring about some sort of change, to cut something out. And in order to do that, I'm going to have to inflict pain."

For Pittman this means that he is most likely to do bad therapy when he inflicts surgical pain at the wrong moment or in the wrong place. "So I have to be very aware of my effect on the people that I am working with."

In spite of this vigilance, Pittman admitted that he made mistakes in every single session that he conducted. "In every interview I am hitting something too hard or not hard enough. I'm hitting the wrong thing or my reality testing is faulty, but even then my caring comes through, and more importantly, my optimism for change."

This reminded him of another example in which he had been seeing two different couples in the same week and he mixed them up. "I had the history completely wrong and the circumstances completely wrong and I was fumbling around not making any sense out of what sort of reactions I was getting. The people I see can read my mind, they know what I'm feeling and thinking, and if I'm confused they get confused too—unless they just dismiss me. I can do some pretty stupid stuff. I can be quite wrong about what I am doing."

Frank paused for dramatic effect and warned us that what was coming next was his key point. "What these massagelike therapists know is that the relationship has got to be comforting and it has to feel safe. That's not the therapy and that's not what's therapeutic, and if you keep people in that position for too long you do them great damage. You drain off their power. You make them dependent upon you."

Pittman admitted that many of his patients derived tremendous comfort from their relationship with him. He doesn't exactly discourage these feelings of being supported because they could be useful for the work that is to follow, but in his view this isn't therapy. Therapy to him is when he pinpoints what people are doing wrong and can do so in a way that they aren't threatened or driven away.

MAKING PEOPLE UNCOMFORTABLE

We asked Pittman what advice he had for other therapists with respect to how they could think about their lousy efforts or process their failures. Without missing a beat, he drove home his earlier point.

"If you are doing strong enough therapy, you'll piss people off sometimes. Bad therapy is the kind that only comforts and massages. It leaves people with all these emotions and no direction. Yet, when you give people a direction and point out their errors, they might not like it. You are going to inflict pain and they may try to escape from it by being angry with you. The fact that they are angry with you does not mean that you are doing bad therapy at all."

As Frank talked about the consequences of doing "good" therapy, and explained further about the inevitability of making people mad, we realized that this long-standing issue continued to limit our own willingness to take more risks along the line that Pittman had suggested.

"So," Jon asked, "you're telling therapists that if they are comfortable they should beware?"

"Exactly," Pittman answered. "If you are comfortable then you probably are not doing what you should be doing."

"Then what does that mean for therapists like me?" Jeffrey asked him, "those of us who have a problem with people being angry at them."

"But that's your job."

"Say more about that," we prompted him.

"Your job is to be a spokesperson for the sort of reality that people's parents and neighbors have been trying to point out to them. They have rejected that reality because somebody didn't love them enough. You have to be a spokesperson for that sort of conventional wisdom, for that sort of honesty. You have got to do it without pissing people off so badly that they will reject you."

We wondered how Pittman managed to be so pit-bullish and get away with it. Was it really that he looks like Elmer Fudd as he so claims? Was it that soft, gentle voice that sounds like a Southern version of Public Radio's Garrison Keiller? Maybe it was his essential caring that came through in spite of his protests about its relative unimportance.

Returning to the earlier case of the man who wanted to be absolved of responsibility for his affair, Pittman remarked: "If he can blame the affair on his wife, or forces within the marriage, then he can relieve his

guilt. My job as a therapist—your job too—is to make people feel sufficient guilt to change but not so much guilt that they will recoil from the
therapy, and not so much guilt that they will personalize it in such a way
that they see themselves as bad or evil."

Pittman's final conclusion about all this: There is no way to do this
sort of work without having people get mad at you. The really hard part,
which he seemed to have mastered, is not to take the anger personally, to
realize it comes with the territory. Of course it is one thing to understand
this intellectually and quite another to internalize it to the point where it
sticks. And then again, in the wrong hands, this could be a recipe for
anyone less skilled and morally grounded to do some pretty crazy things
to people all in the name of pissing them off therapeutically.

"Knowing these things," Pittman was asked next, "when was the
last time that you violated your own rule and did bad therapy because of
your own need to be liked and your unwillingness to make people angry?"

"If I render myself harmless enough, and warm enough, and huggy
enough, I can tell people just about anything I want. And I can do it in a
way that won't make them see me as their attacker—most of the time.
Some do see me as the attacker, no matter what I do, and if they are
determined to see me that way, at least I want to do a kamikaze maneu-
ver in which I go out as the therapist with a clear message, with an ines-
capable message of what useful action they have the power to take."

Pittman returned to the first case of the young guy who lived with
the six women. "That kid left but he knew very clearly what was expected of him and he knew there was at least one person who believed he
was capable of doing it. I don't know how things turned out in the end.
How it turned out depended on all sort of things over which I had no
control. I try my hardest not to take responsibility for things over which
I have no control—that would really paralyze me as a therapist. It's a
tough thing for a therapist to do because basically we are such sweet,
loving people. We just want to nurture people like those six women did
with that dependent kid."

"One final question, Frank. How would you like us to introduce
you?"

"I've been around about as long as anyone in family therapy. Because I have been doing private practice most of that time, and because I
am rather a terminal workaholic, I've done a lot of family therapy. I
figured recently I had logged more than 75,000 hours. And I'm still not
doing it right."

Chapter 13

SAM GLADDING
I Zigged When I Should Have Zagged

With his delicate features and constant smile, SAM GLADDING is easily approachable. Add to the mix a soft North Carolina accent and a relaxed, easy-going manner, and you would never guess that he has been a university administrator for the past decade. He looks more like a preschool teacher. The only giveaway that he works with grown-ups, and especially those at the highest levels of university administration, is his immaculate appearance.

Sam Gladding has authored several of the major texts in the counseling profession, including *Community and Agency Counseling, The Counseling Dictionary, Counseling: A Comprehensive Profession, Family Therapy: History, Theory, and Practice, Group Work: A Counseling Specialty, Ethical, Legal, Professional Issues in the Practice of Marriage and Family Therapy*, and *Becoming a Counselor: The Light, the Bright, and the Serious.*

Gladding has been a professor of counseling at Wake Forest University, Winston-Salem, North Carolina, for much of his working life, and before that, a practitioner in a variety of settings. He has served in a number of administrative positions within his university as assistant to the president, and within the profession as President of the Association for Counselor Education and Supervision. Throughout many of his later years, he has concentrated on the creative process in the practice of therapy, authoring a book on the subject (*Counseling as an Art*), and also practicing what he preaches by inserting his playful spirit into conversations.

Although Gladding reported that he found the prospect of talking about his failures quite difficult, he actually sounded eager and excited to talk about the subject. He also remained uncharacteristically serious throughout the conversation, as if the subject was so important that he didn't want to diminish it with his often humorous observations.

ANTICIPATION

Since one of Sam Gladding's signatures is to insert song lyrics from the 1960s and 1970s into his comments, and then wait with a mischievous glint in his eye to see if the listener notices what he's done, it seemed only fitting that we name the first section after the title of Carly Simon's song of the same name. We began our conversation by asking Sam about what he had been thinking about in anticipation of this interview.

"Actually," he answered with a soft laugh, "I've been anticipating having a rather bad time." He paused for a moment, making sure we understood his play on words related to the subject under discussion, and then continued. "Realistically I've really thought that this would be a good chance for a learning experience. It gives me a chance to reflect on situations that have not turned out ideally because all too often we read about and talk about only those things that go right and kind of cover up the other."

"So," we began, jumping right into things, "what is bad therapy to you?"

"I've thought about that on two levels," Gladding responded. It was obvious that he was well prepared for the questions we intended to cover. "On a professional level it is when either the therapist or client displays inappropriate or less than desirable behavior that results in a bad situation. On a more personal level, it is when I do or say something in therapy that doesn't succeed. I feel inept." For Sam, the feeling about the way things are going (or not going) is at least as important as the objective outcome.

We moved immediately to the realm of personal failures in his work. Rather than asking him the question he most expected, that is, what case would he like to talk about, instead we asked him about the one counseling situation which he had most wanted to avoid.

Without hesitation, he replied: "I must confess that it is a situation that I haven't thought about in a very long time. This was a middle-aged woman who complained about being nervous all the time. I tried to help her relax so we could begin working on her situation. Not only was I unsuccessful in helping her to calm down, but she actually became even more agitated. She kept asking if she could leave. Finally, she just bolted out of the office and ran."

ENDURING FEELINGS

Knowing that his feelings about his work are so important, the next question was obvious: "So, what was that like for you?"

"It was horrible! I tried everything I could think of and nothing worked. I did whatever I could do and it still wasn't enough." Sensing the pain and helplessness of his memory, all we could think to do was repeat what he had just said, simply repeating his own words.

"Yeah," Gladding answered with real sadness in his voice. "I tried systematic desensitization. I tried to work on her irrational thinking. I went with deep breathing. I asked her to try meditation. But nothing worked. She just got worse and worse."

Just as curious to us about which cases our interviewees select as the worst examples of their work, are their judgments about why those particular cases are so lousy. In Sam's case, we asked him what he found so indefensible in his own behavior. After all, it seemed apparent that this was a rather challenging situation that almost any therapist would have trouble with.

Sam agreed with this assessment but he refused to let himself off the hook. "I just didn't prepare her well for what we were going to do. I probably tried going too fast in the session rather than being reflective and letting her talk a bit more. Rather than letting her talk, I kept trying to fix her. I just felt awful. I felt like I zigged when I should have zagged. If that makes any sense." Excited about the descriptive metaphor he had just introduced, we prodded him to explain more about what he meant.

"Maybe I should have been more self-disclosing and personal with her, especially about my own nervousness. I certainly should have reflected her feelings more often and stayed with her experience. Maybe that would have been more appropriate instead of going with a 'Let's see if I can help you relax' kind of response."

SECOND GUESSES

There was no shortage of response options that Gladding could think of now that he could have done instead. He went through what he did systematically, checking off each behavior and its ineffectual response, and then reflected on what he might have done instead. Although this case occurred over two decades ago, he still recalled every detail as if this woman were still part of his current caseload.

We asked him about this very observation. Why was it that after all these years, and all the people he had worked with, that *this* was the case that stood out most? We were curious as to why he picked this example instead of another that might have been more dramatic or life-threatening. There was obviously something about this woman in particular that really hit his feelings of ineptitude.

"I think she's the only person I've ever had who literally walked out on me. And she did it so quickly! I don't think we were in the session even 20 minutes before she ended it rather abruptly. I just didn't connect with her on any level. And the worst part of this for me was that it looked like such an easy case. I thought to myself that it would be simple to help her, not much of a challenge at all. And then there was no closure. I never discovered what happened."

"So, then, what did you learn from this experience?"

"The first thing is to go slow sometimes. I think up to that point in my career I was pretty confident and pretty self-assured. I knew I wasn't perfect but I felt pretty good going into most situations. I thought here is a situation that is maybe teaching me that there is much more to human life than what I thought I knew. Instead of addressing matters as quickly as I had before, I've been more cautious and more humble in working with people."

Since Gladding is about the most humble, modest, and self-deprecating person we know, we wondered if this incident was not critical in shaping who he was today. Frankly, it was difficult to imagine him as arrogant or overconfident.

PEARLS OF WISDOM

It was Gladding's hope that others could learn from his experience that regardless of a situation, no matter how simple and predictable things appear to be, one must be prepared for the unexpected. One of the dangers for a veteran is in treating new cases as if they are all familiar, as if we've seen and done it all before. We can then fail to see what might really be unfolding because our own assumptions are getting in the way.

For Gladding being a therapist is being a lifelong learner. "It's being somebody who's constantly trying to understand the human condition. It is about realizing that people sometimes don't fit our theories." Since this episode was so impactful and educational for Gladding, we asked his thoughts about why we are all so reluctant to talk about our screw-ups and failures.

"I think there are at least two reasons: One is that counseling is somewhat of a lonely profession; I mean that only in the sense that we are there, the client is there, and yet because of confidentiality we don't speak about many things that occur in the therapeutic session. Even in supervision we kind of keep it to ourselves. Second, to admit these mistakes probably causes us to lose some status."

Gladding admitted that once a therapist has achieved a certain status in the field, being a well-known writer and speaker, there is even more to lose. It is as if we have superhuman expectations of ourselves, so that we begin to believe in our own myths.

Before the discussion was brought to a close, Gladding was quick to point out that this was hardly the only case of bad therapy that he'd had; it was just the one that haunted him the most. "I think that bad experiences in therapy are like grains of sand in oysters. At first, they are really irritating. They can even kill us. But over time, if we live long enough, they can become pearls of wisdom."

Chapter 14

SUSAN M. JOHNSON
I Felt Quite Helpless

SUSAN JOHNSON was instrumental in developing one of the first systematic brief forms of couples therapy. Integrating facets of humanistic and systemic concepts, emotionally focused therapy (EFT) seeks to help couples to express themselves emotionally in constructive ways.

Johnson's books on therapy blend a solid research base with an experiential approach that helps practitioners to proceed step-by-step to help troubled couples to access their concerns and issues, and communicate these thoughts and feelings in productive, enhancing ways. Most importantly, Johnson believes that key attachment-related emotions, when elicited and clearly expressed, can evoke new responses in partners and facilitate more secure bonding.

In her books, *Emotionally Focused Therapy for Couples*, *The Practice of Emotionally Focused Therapy: Creating Connection*, and *The Heart of the Matter: Perspectives on Emotion in Psychotherapy*, Johnson has provided clinicians with a blueprint that allows them to proceed in consistently helpful ways to conflicted couples.

Johnson is Professor of Psychology at Ottawa University, Ontario, Canada and Director of the Ottawa Couple and Family Institute. The website for EFT is www.eft.ca

MAGICAL GURUS

Johnson began by talking about her reactions to working on this project with us. She felt that looking at bad therapy was incredibly important and wondered why this was not done more often, especially by the field's leaders.

"The thing about magical gurus is that they can always come up with magic and that they never just go in and struggle in a session and make boo boos. I think that is very bad for what we do because I think it somehow creates our field as magical theater rather than an ongoing learning process. We are mentors who have gone through our own learning. This gives other people permission to learn and it gives us continual permission to learn. I feel like one of the reasons I do couples therapy is because I learn from every couple."

Johnson paused for a moment. "Of course the issue is what you see as a mistake is going to depend on your model. If I watch a solution-focused therapist from my point of view, this whole approach is a mistake because for me it is superficial. It's not really addressing the heart of the matter. That's my own bias, of course."

Susan again reviewed her experiences as a clinician, teacher, and supervisor, still struggling with which case she could talk about that might be most instructive. We suggested that she might begin by looking at the one that still haunted her the most.

FAILING TO CONNECT

"The essence of EFT is that you try to empathically connect with your client. That allows you to create safety, as well as a secure bond where that client can explore things that they wouldn't normally explore. One of the clear mistakes in this model is then to become stuck in blaming and pathologizing people. In EFT terms, that would be the biggest mistake of all. The only way out of that situation that I know is to be able to set aside the stance of magical expert. This means being able to say to someone that 'I am very sorry but I don't understand the position you are taking in this relationship at the moment. Can you help me? Is it like this . . . ?'"

Johnson said that this position was especially challenging when clients were angry or disappointed. In such situations, therapists may try even harder to present themselves as omnipotent experts who are to be respected without question. This point reminded her of the case she wanted to talk about.

"I remember one lady who stormed into my office and announced that she thought all therapists were incompetent. I was the ninth one she had seen and I was probably going to be incompetent as well."

To make matters worse, Johnson was feeling tired and depleted as the session began. When this prevailing fatigue was coupled with the difficulty connecting with the client, there was clearly a problem that was not going to be easily resolved.

"The woman sat in my office and very aggressively berated her husband who was obviously totally intimidated by her. She basically told me a story about the fact that her husband was completely callous and incompetent. To prove her point, she had told him during a past fight that he was so ineffectual that he wouldn't even be able to be there for her if she was dying. She had then told him that the relationship was over. She then described how she had pretended to hang herself. She went and got a rope and told him she was going to hang herself. She then went down to the basement and made all the noises that would give the impression that she had hanged herself. She timed how long it took him to come down to the basement—it took him 10 minutes. This proved then how useless he was."

Susan was appalled by this test. She was even more frustrated because the woman kept interrupting her—at one point, even yelling at her.

"I'm tired and it's hot and this lady says this to me. I started to say blaming things to her. I started to say things like, 'You really felt like you needed to go to this extreme measure,' and 'You were trying to prove him wrong.'"

Johnson knew this was not particularly helpful but she felt powerless to stop the communication pattern that had developed between them. After the session ended, she thought more and more about what happened and felt very uneasy about the way she had handled things and how she had lost her perspective and her ability to put herself in this woman's shoes.

"In my head I started linking her behavior to different personality disorders. Then I realized I was in real trouble because my whole model depends on being able to put myself in the place of a client and expand this client's experience by bringing in key marginalized elements."

Instead of trying to figure out a way to connect with her client, Johnson found herself trying to find a nasty label to assign to her diagnosis, as if this would let her off the hook. After all, if she was borderline or narcissistic then surely Johnson would have a legitimate excuse for failing to develop a solid alliance.

"It took me until about 11 at night and then I don't know what happened. Sometimes it just takes time. Suddenly it was like I could hear her voice without getting reactive myself and without getting caught in a negative cycle myself with her. I was just able to hear what she said. Somehow it felt like I had got it. Then I was able to go in the next time and repair what I'm sure was a rift in the alliance. I was able to say to her that I was so sorry that I didn't understand her. I had started blaming and labeling her because I didn't understand."

Realizing how she had failed to make an authentic empathic connection, Susan tried her best to communicate her new understanding. She said to the woman:

"What I didn't understand until I put myself in your shoes was what incredible courage it must have taken to test out your worst fears. You were so afraid and you were saying to your husband, 'I can't count on you in the most basic ways. I believe that you would abandon me if I was dying.' That is a huge thing to say. And the fact is that you felt the need to actually put yourself in a situation where you tested that, even though this might have looked a little bizarre to somebody from the outside. I can't imagine how much pain you must have been in and also how much courage it must have taken to really test it. The conclusion you came up with is that he really couldn't be there for you. If indeed that is true, then the relationship really isn't safe for you."

Johnson disclosed to the woman how humbled she felt hearing her story. She told her that she would never have had the courage to do the same thing. Once Johnson stopped judging the woman and simply tried to understand her, the relationship blossomed.

"When I validated her, when I was able to connect with her, to my surprise she turned suddenly into this coherent, logical lady who was struggling with her grief and trying to accept that the man she had married in a shipboard romance really could not be a spouse to her. She burst into tears."

"Yes," the woman admitted. "I know he can't be there for me. He was a bachelor and a loner all his life. I'm trying to move to the point where I see him as a friend. I can't count on him. It's not his fault. He doesn't really want to have a partner. I kind of captured him."

Johnson was fascinated by the dramatic transformation that took place, all the result of the more empathic stance. "I still keep that in my head as a lesson. You can't tell what people are capable of when they walk into your office. Sometimes they look bizarre, or developmentally delayed, personality disordered, unskilled, immature, aggressive—they look like all these things. But you are seeing them at their most vulnerable, when they have their toes hanging over a cliff. In those circumstances we are all a little strange."

For Johnson felt she was most likely to get in trouble with her clients when she started to label them, blame them, judge them. "Bad therapy for me involves times when I get caught in a reactive cycle with clients and start to pathologize them and not give them the benefit of the doubt. If I had then started to do some sort of superficial coaching, trying to teach her not to be so aggressive, I think it would have been even worse."

Johnson observed that when things go wrong there is a great temptation for therapists to blame their clients. Of course, the reason some clients come to therapy in the first place is because they may have difficulty connecting or have a way of engaging others that is perceived as challenging.

NOT MUCH I COULD DO

In spite of her desire to talk about mistakes in an open way, we noticed that this particular case of bad therapy was quickly reversed by the next session. What about another time when she didn't realize what she was doing wrong so quickly, and wasn't able to fix things? She thought immediately about one couple she tried to help. She was stumped and felt stuck, unsure how to adapt her model in a way to break through the impasse.

"I remember one man who was exceedingly verbally abusive to his wife. According to the EFT model, I tried to contain that negative emotion. I was able to hold it and I was able to put it in the context of his attachment, his needs and fears, and I was able to put it in the context of interactional cycles. I was then able to help a client like him look at how he created the relationship, and the impact he was having on his spouse, and to take some responsibility, and begin to go beyond all this anger. I wanted him to be able to talk about other emotions, such as his insecurities, which might then open up new ways for him to connect with his partner. That is how it is supposed to work in theory. In the cold reality of the first few sessions, however, things weren't proceeding at all according to plan.

"I just couldn't get the husband to take any responsibility. Every time we would get to a certain spot and I would point out what he was doing, he would blame his wife and justify his behavior. I would then feel the need to protect his partner. Of course, if this goes on and you can't shift this abusive behavior, it is a contraindication for couples therapy."

Johnson now questioned whether she should even be working with this couple. She began to push harder to get the husband into shifting his rigid, controlling stance. "He would turn and call his wife dreadful names and I would say, 'I'm sorry, but you can't talk to your wife like that here.' That's when we would get stuck and he would get very hostile with me. He would not allow me to explore his experience or comment on his behavior."

Johnson arrived at the conclusion that this was just not a good case for couples therapy. The man needed to examine his rage, and yet do so in a setting that was less volatile and more safe. Although she reassured herself that there was little else she could have done, Susan wondered if there were other ways she could have reached him.

"One of the reasons I ask that is because it was pretty clear to me right in that first session that his wife wasn't going to leave him. She really worried me. She looked very depressed. What happened was he got up and stormed off at the end of the session and I was left feeling very worried about this lady. So I tried to talk to her about what had happened. I was worried about her and asked permission to talk to her individual therapist. She listened to me very quietly and wept and then told me that she did not wish me to do this. She was grateful for my empathy but I felt quite helpless."

In this case Johnson felt she didn't do much to help the couple. She couldn't find a way to reach them in spite of her best efforts. She resonated with the couple's own sense of helplessness about changing their interactions. Like the previous example, she felt that this was another instance when she was unable to join successfully with her clients.

COMPLEXITY AND AMBIGUITY

It is one our myths that if we are smart enough, if we study and work hard enough, if we get better training and supervision, if we log enough hours of practice, then we can always figure out what is going on with our clients. If we can't do this while the therapy is going on, then surely we will do so upon reflection. The reality is far more complex: many times we really don't know what happened, much less what went wrong and what our own role was in the failure.

When we asked Johnson what she had learned from this episode, she responded with characteristic honesty. "You know, I just don't know. When you learn something, you say to yourself: Now I know what else I could have done. But in this case, I don't know what else I could have done with that couple. I tried everything I knew to reach him, including trying to show him that he was shooting himself in the foot. When someone can't empathize with his partner, you try somehow to reach his longings and needs—his self-interest and point out how he hurts himself with his behavior. But this man. . . . " Susan's voice trailed off in frustration. She was still wracking her brain trying to unravel the complexity of what had happened. The answer still seemed to elude her, even after so many years.

"I was never quite sure why he had come in the first place. If you can't figure out how to get someone to connect with you and attune to them, then you can't find a way to stand beside him—be in his corner. The bottom line is that I couldn't make an alliance with him and the therapy never got off the ground."

Johnson's answer was unsatisfying, mostly to herself. But rarely are any of us asked to account for ourselves about the worst examples of our work. We sweep them under the rug. We pretend they didn't happen. We blame the client for being resistant or unmotivated or difficult or obstructive or too impaired. The truth of the matter is that a lot of the time we really don't understand what happened and why.

WHAT TO TAKE FROM THIS

Johnson was next asked what others might learn from her experience. Her answer was concise and to the point: You can't do couples therapy when one partner is abusive and is unable or unwilling to contain the negative affect. Defining success in a more limited way, Johnson believed that if only she could have gotten him to see that he had a problem, that might have been an important first step.

"But I couldn't get him there. I think one of the real difficulties for our field is how do you work with a relationship that is so negative and so destructive that you have to start containing every move and breaking each interaction down into bits? How can you change a process when you can't let it unfold?

"It is so hard to accept the limits of what we can do. Sometimes it almost seems that if only we would try a little harder then maybe that would be the breakthrough. But in such cases we may already be trying way too hard, taking on far too much responsibility for an outcome that is ultimately determined by the client."

Johnson tried everything she could with this man. At one point she tried to get him to take a risk with his wife, to show her anything but the cold hostility and emotional abuse he was consistently dishing out. She tried to create an enactment, where he would confide in his spouse, just to see if he could do it. Yet in 20 years of doing this type of work, this was the only time that the client would not comply, would not even try it.

"Oh," Susan challenged him, "so that would be too difficult for you to tell her that? That isn't your usual style. You're not comfortable. Could you tell her that you are not comfortable talking to her about your softer feelings?"

Johnson said that this almost always works, cutting back the expectation to something that anyone could do. She asked him to take a step forward and he said no, so she asked him to move an inch. "This man leaned back in his chair, looked at me, and said no. 'If I do that I am starting to do what it is I just said I would not do, aren't I ?'" Johnson agreed.

In her EFT model, Johnson believes that if someone cannot or will not make a shift, then it is best to back up to where they are and stay with them for a while and recognize their stuckness and need to protect themselves and validate this until they can take a step forward. In this case, however, this was not possible .

"Nobody had ever totally refused this kind of intervention before. It was totally frustrating. I am used to this working. It was sort of like, 'Oh! You won't move at all!' Here is the issue: I've had clients say this in other ways, like 'I can't move at all,' and you can work with that. You say, 'Oh, you can't move at all.' And you just reflect that: as in 'Can you turn to your wife and say, I can't let you in. I don't think I can ever let you in. Perhaps I'm never going to let anyone in.' You can work with that. Somehow, when they say it, and actively take their incredibly stuck position, my experience is that they move. With this guy, though, that wasn't an option because his position was that he had the right to stand and massacre his partner, which I could not validate. I couldn't let him do that; I couldn't watch him do that. His position was that she was pathetic and that he had the right to stand back here and define her in that demeaning way. I couldn't validate that. I couldn't even allow him to sit there in front of me wounding her. If I had allowed that I would have been condoning his behavior."

So the lesson from this that Susan Johnson mentioned is that bad therapy takes place not only when your model doesn't work, but when you don't have another model that you can reach for. You see that clients need something other than what you are offering them, but you can't figure out what that might be. You remain stuck with what you already know how to do.

Chapter 15

PAT LOVE
Listening to My Inner Voice

One of the first things you notice about PAT LOVE is her voice, a commanding yet playful instrument that is laced with traces of West Virginia, Texas, and other places she has lived. The early stages of her career were devoted to teaching marriage and family therapy, first at Texas A & M University, Commerce, and later at private training institutes. More recently, Love has written several successful books for couples including *Hot Monogamy, The Intimate Couple, Handbook for the Soul*, and *The Truth About Love*.

UNDER MY SKIN

When she thought about bad therapy, that is, the kind that wasn't especially helpful to a client, Pat Love recalled the case of a young woman referred to her from a university counseling center. The 21 year old had been attending school out of state but was forced to take a leave of absence after an unsuccessful suicide attempt.

The distraught student spent time recovering in an inpatient unit, ending up in the care of Love as part of her after-treatment care. "I worked with her on several issues," she recalled. "Since the source of many of her problems, and much of her distress, stemmed from family of origin issues I suggested we invite her family in to talk about some things."

Love nodded her head in remembrance, the details of the case becoming clearer as she told the story. "The woman was more than a little reluctant, even frightened, at the prospect of conducting sessions with the whole family present. She seemed particularly concerned about her father being part of the process since he was so controlling and dogmatic. This was obviously a very complex, ambivalent relationship in that she was both terrified of the man, as well as being irresistibly attracted to him. It was almost like a traumatic bonding between them."

In analyzing the situation, Pat saw this as a case of a young adult trying to differentiate herself from a dysfunctional situation at home. The father was trying to hold onto her. The mother was somewhat weak and passive, but overinvolved with the younger children who were also acting out. Ironically, the student's suicide attempt landed her back in the same situation she had tried so hard to escape.

Recognizing a somewhat classical pattern, Love knew that, somehow, she had to get the family involved in the treatment if she was ever going to help the young woman to move on with her life. Yet when she attempted to get the parents and other siblings to join the therapy, the father was the only one who agreed to attend.

"This was my first mistake," Pat said with a wistful expression. "If I had worked with the whole family there would have been a more balanced point of view. But when the father came in, he was incredibly angry. He was even more controlling than my client had described. And his anger was not only directed toward his daughter who had frightened, embarrassed, and disappointed him, but also at me. This I did not like at all."

When the father and daughter returned home after the session, they immediately got into a big argument. The father launched into his usual controlling behavior, the only recourse for the daughter being that she had to escape: She stormed out of the house and went to stay with her boyfriend. It was at this point that the father called Love and instructed her to fix the mess that he claimed she had created. "He actually wanted me to go to the boyfriend's house, retrieve his daughter, and bring her home. Well, I explained to him that this wasn't part of my job." Love shook her head, thinking about this guy who so easily got underneath her skin.

Love's unwillingness to put herself under the father's complete control only enraged the man further. "He called me every name he could think of. He maligned me as a woman, and as a professional—I don't know which hurt worse. He threatened to sue me. I was just stunned. And I was scared."

Love now knew exactly what her client felt like, although she would never have chosen to find out in precisely this way. She tried her best to stay calm. She reflected back the strong feelings that she heard pouring out of the phone. She tried to deflect his anger and interpret the source of his helplessness. In response to each of her attempts to make contact with him, the man replied, "I am not your client. Don't speak to me that way." Pat was frustrated and exasperated, at a loss as to how to proceed next. "One thing was clear to me: there was no way I was going to invite this guy back into therapy. Once I resolved to keep the man away from my relationship with the young woman, I felt much better."

Eventually, Love helped the student to stabilize her situation. "I probably did a fair job," she said, not at all convincing, even to herself. "In truth, I felt like I had lost all my effectiveness."

LOSING CONTROL

As she looked back on the case, Pat realized that she did not handle things well at all. Her client had given her fair warning that the father was a powder keg of anger, yet she did not take adequate steps to anticipate and manage his outbursts. Somehow, she thought she could charm him, or win him over; she believed her skills and experience would protect her. She had been overconfident. And she let herself get sucked into a power struggle with the one person who thrived on that sort of battle. "I neither protected my client very well, nor defended myself constructively. It became so important for me to stand up to him, to be a model for my client who was so terrified of the guy. Ultimately, he scared me as well."

In making sense of how and why she misjudged this case, Love realized that there was some pretty strong countertransference feelings going on related to her own stepfather. "It was like I went into an altered state. I think I disassociated, to be honest with you. I was just so caught off guard, so blindsided, that I lost control of myself and my work."

Looking thoughtful, Love recalled a similar instance in which she had also lost control. What was different, however, was that she had a solid relationship with the man so she was able to work things through in a constructive way. Because she had never taken the time to establish any rapport with this father, however, there was little she could do to salvage things, or even regain her dignity.

"A lot of the problem was that I didn't feel safe with him. I felt very much like my client. I wondered if he might hurt me physically. And I had no doubt that he would try to hurt me professionally." Once she felt afraid and let herself be put on the defensive, Love found she lost her effectiveness. In trying to put things in perspective, Love was brutally honest with herself about things she did wrong. "I just dropped the ball. I didn't help my client. I didn't help the family. And I fell deep into my own issues."

Typical of most highly skilled and self-demanding practitioners, Love is unduly hard on herself. In reality, the young woman did make some progress and ended up referred back to the counseling center on campus, and she eventually resumed her studies. Nevertheless, this was not good work by any stretch of the imagination. Any progress the client made was most likely in spite of the therapy rather than because of it. What are the lessons to be learned from this case?

"Well, for one thing, if you have posttraumatic stress yourself you should be careful about getting into similar territory with clients. Second, I realize now that I made a big mistake by not getting the whole family involved in the therapy. I could have diluted the man's anger with others present. Instead, it ended up a struggle for power, one that I lost."

TRUSTING INTUITION

The bigger issue for Love had to do with not trusting her intuition. All along, she sensed that it was not advisable to work with the father and daughter alone, but she ignored her inner voice. "This wasn't just about the two of them. It was a family issue. I knew that but I ignored what I was feeling."

Love didn't listen to her clinical wisdom, she ignored what she was feeling, and she became overconfident. Pat admitted that she could have gotten supervision around this. She should have recognized that her own issues might become involved in a case like this in which she was overidentifying with her client. "It's just that I was caught off guard. I just don't do well when someone is yelling at me."

This was the first time that something like this had happened in Love's work. She was unprepared to manage the case because what was required was not within her repertoire at the time. Her intuition might have been telling her what to do but she wasn't sure how to make it happen.

"The really interesting thing to me about this situation was that my client wasn't surprised at all by what happened. She had told me what he was like but I ignored her warnings. I figured I'd show her how it was done. When the father and I had started going after one another, my client just sat there as though it was business as usual. She'd seen this all many times before."

Love let herself become triangulated between the father and daughter. "This was just another piece of the drama that they enacted continuously. They already knew the rules and the steps of the dance. I was the naive bystander who let herself get sucked into it."

Love stopped the narrative at this point. "I wish I could remember more, but frankly I've blocked a lot of this out." She seemed uncharacteristically apologetic and wondered if this story was the kind of thing we were looking for. Before she got an answer, Love chuckled to herself. "I told you the story, didn't I, the one about my friend who fell asleep in session? Just as he jerked his head up, resuming consciousness, he heard his client say, 'And *that's* something I've never told anybody in my whole life.'"

Pat's rich laugh was contagious so it wasn't hard to lighten up over this painfully serious subject. But even through the banter and jokes that came afterwards, it was clear that she was still haunted by this case of the woman she couldn't help, and the father who got underneath her skin.

Chapter 16

ART FREEMAN
We're Not as Smart
as We Think We Are

ARTHUR FREEMAN is one of the most active and articulate voices in the cognitive behavioral movement, especially as applied to personality disorders. He is the author of over 25 books that apply cognitive therapy to various specialty areas including pain management, personality disorders, suicidal behaviors, children and adolescents, and borderline personality disorder. He has also written two books for the public applying cognitive therapy principles to everyday life: *Woulda, Coulda, Shoulda: Overcoming Regrets, Mistakes, and Missed Opportunities* and *The 10 Dumbest Mistakes Smart People Make and How to Avoid Them.*

Freeman is Professor and Chair of Psychology at the Philadelphia College of Osteopathic Medicine.

ONE OF US SHOULD KNOW WHAT WE'RE DOING

Since Art has specialized throughout his career in working with very difficult clients who present intractable personality disorders and other chronic conditions, we expected that he would have more than his fair share of war stories to share with us. Given his areas of clinical specialty, we wondered how he defined bad therapy.

"That would mean that there were significant impediments to the therapy work that I didn't account for," he said. "My basic premise is that if there are two people in the consulting room, one of them should have an idea of where they are going." Freeman talked about how many therapists were often trained in the nondirective tradition to follow the client's lead because he or she is supposed to know where to go. "I don't think that's true," Freeman said, "because if clients knew where they were going they wouldn't be in therapy in the first place. They would be going someplace that would be far more fun."

THE WORST ONE IS REALLY TOUGH

We asked Freeman to select an example of what he considered his worst example of therapy and he wondered if it had to be his absolute worst or just "a lousy one." It was clear he was still debating about whether to talk about a particular case or not. With a deep breath, he began the story.

"Gerald was a 16-year-old boy who was referred by his school for therapy. The reason for the referral was that he had a significant motor tic that involved head shaking. The other kids called him 'Twitch.' According to the school, there was no medical or neurological explanation for the tic. He also was reported to be isolated. Freeman explained that although the boy was an excellent student and gifted learner, he was friendless in school and in his neighborhood."

After meeting with Gerald for a half-hour, Freeman met with Gerald's parents. In the first interview with the boy's parents, he saw that they were extremely concerned about their son but reluctant to place him in therapy. They were very clear that they had come for therapy only at the insistence of Gerald's guidance counselor.

Freeman asked a number of questions regarding Gerald's development and present life. When he questioned Gerald's lack of friends, the mother said, "He'll have plenty of time later to make friends. He's really got to do well in high school so he can get into a good college and then go to law school. "Are you aware of this head-shaking thing that he does?" Freeman asked them.

"Yes," the mother answered. "So what? My brother owns a successful lamp business and he does the same kind of thing. He's married and has kids. Who cares? Gerald will be fine."

"Are you aware that the kids make fun of him and that he seems to have no friends?" Freeman asked. The mother made a face and didn't respond to that question. Finally, at the end of the meeting, Freeman asked the mother and father if they had any questions of him.

"Yes, as a matter of fact, I do," said the father.

"Thank God," Freeman thought to himself. The father hadn't said a word up until that point.

"First question. In the waiting room, you have some very nice music playing. What radio station is that?" Freeman was astonished.

"And your next question?" Freeman asked. The man looked around the office, scanning the floor-to-ceiling bookshelves and asked, "Have you read all these books?"

"Those were his only questions," Art said to us. The next session involved meeting with Gerald. "Gerald was at first reluctant to speak and told me that he didn't think that he needed to come to see me. When I asked him why he thought that he said because his mother was very clear that therapy was a waste of time. He came in for the session by himself, traveling by bus and subway to get to the office. By the second session, Gerald was speaking quite freely. He really wanted to talk and seemed to relish the opportunity to unburden himself. He would talk about his lack of friends, and while he echoed his mother's statement that his goal was to get good grades so that he could get into a good college, and then do well in college so that he could get into a good law school, he also was feeling very alone and isolated. He had two sisters, 15 and 13 years old. They all shared a bedroom in a home where there was no need to do that. They could each have had their own room but the mother said it was better if they all slept in one room so it would be easier for her to clean and to make the beds."

Freeman thought, "Here is a kid who probably wanted to stick his hands in his pants at night and he's got two sisters sleeping in the same room with him. Gerald also said it described a situation that could best be labeled as a game called 'I dropped the towel.' His 15-year-old sister would come out of the shower into the bedroom, while Gerald was there, with a towel on her head and another towel around her body, and say, 'Oh, I dropped my towel.' He would look and she'd always have her back to him and he would see her bare butt."

"As Gerald would describe this 'game' his head shaking would increase. Given the lack of any medical basis, I thought that this was clearly an anxiety problem. The kid was anxious all of the time. My conceptualization was he had no way of releasing the anxiety. He did not play sports, he did not exercise, and he did not masturbate. I saw this muscle twitch as a manifestation of severe anxiety. He had no more cognitive ways of relieving his anxiety, so he just suffered with it."

Based on this reading of the situation, Freeman talked to the boy about how he might arrange to release a lot of his nervous energy, and, just as importantly, how he might create some privacy for himself. They figured out that he could use the room, now used as Gerald's "study," as his own bedroom. They also talked about how to present this idea to his mother in such a way that it would give him more time to study late at night without waking his sisters. His explanation was that there might be times that he would want to get up and study in the middle of the night and he could do that if he had his own room. He also promised that he would make his bed and keep the room clean.

"His mother bought the idea," Freeman said, "so that part of the problem-solution seemed to work. An administrative problem emerged though, and that was that the parents were not paying the fees for the sessions. At the initial session they had told me that they didn't have a lot of money (although they were hardly poor since both of them were working.) I set the fee at a level that I considered modest and to which they agreed ($50.00 per session). By the end of six sessions I hadn't gotten a penny so I called the parents to find out what was going on.

"Your check must be lost in the mail," the mother said.

"Given that it has been some time since you sent the check, it might make sense to stop payment on that check and issue me another check? In fact, why don't you just give the check to Gerald and ask him to bring it in with him to the next session."

Although the parents agreed to do just that, it didn't happen. The boy showed up to the session without the payment. Again, Freeman called the parents to find out what the problem was, and again the mother said that she would take care of the bill. Another two weeks elapsed and still no payment. Finally, Art called a third time and told them that unless they paid the bill he would be unable to see their son any longer, but would refer him to the community mental health center. Gerald's mother replied that she did not want her son being seen at the community mental health center. She also pointed out that the bill for therapy was now $600 and that since they were a poor family, $600 was a great deal of money for them.

"I should mention at this point that once Gerald got his own room and started masturbating regularly and vigorously, his symptoms decreased markedly. He still had a neck-stretching motion that he learned to combine with a shoulder shrug that now looked as if he was simply stretching tight muscles. The progress was remarkable and dramatic."

When Gerald came in for his next session he was trembling. His head shaking was back full tilt. When I asked him what was going on, he told me that that morning his mother had taken him to the bank and said, "I have to pay your therapist. This is money that will never be replaced. This is money for your college." She then withdrew $600 in $100 bills, gave it to Gerald, and made him put it in his sock in case he was mugged on the bus.

"Gerald was anxious as hell. He was afraid he was going to lose the family money. He walked in and said, 'I have something for you.' He took off his shoe and his sock, and gave me 6 sopping wet $100 bills. They were soaked. His tic was back to the pretherapy level. He had nothing to talk about, and wanted to leave immediately. He then got up, despite my encouragement to stay, and he left. He never came back again."

UNDERESTIMATING POWER

Without prompting him to talk about the mistake he had made, Freeman immediately explained that he had underestimated, and did not properly take into account, the mother's power. "Most simply, I did not get her to join in the effort. I should have paid homage to her power and gotten her to join with me. By not doing that, I then allowed her to sabotage the therapy. In thinking about it afterwards, I wondered why I didn't. I was experienced, and I knew better. The only explanation I could offer is that, well, I was angry with her. I was annoyed with her. I felt her business of making all the beds at once was crazy. The kids could have made their own beds. Even if they didn't make their beds, why was that such a major issue? I was annoyed at the way she treated her husband and talked to him too. I was angry at the way she was manipulating me with the session fee.

"But this was all in retrospect as I thought about what I could have done differently. I was just angry with her and that really clouded what I did with the kid. I was just so pleased I was able to help this kid so quickly I didn't pay enough attention to his environment."

So, what did Art learn from this episode, we asked him. "I have a model of resistance. I have a list of 48 issues that act as impediments to therapy, each one stemming from roughly four main areas: (1) those from the patient, which we generally call *resistance*; (2) those from the environment, which we generally label *sabotage*; (3) those from the pathology itself (e.g., you don't expect depressed people to have a lot of energy); and (4) those from the therapist, which are usually the result of therapeutic errors or of countertransference."

Although Freeman was fully aware of these concepts, he was blind to his own negative personal reactions. "I was aware that the mother was a powerful character but I underestimated her power. At the same time, I overestimated my own power because Gerald responded so well to me."

Freeman remembered what the mother said to him in their very first meeting. "My children come to me with every problem," she said. "There is nothing that they can't talk to me about. I talk to my children about everything, about their friends, about everything. I even talk to them about masturbation."

At this point Art remembered thinking that she was incredibly intrusive and controlling. She pushed his buttons to the point where he ignored the power that she wielded to sabotage the therapy. Ever since that time he has worked hard to make sure he doesn't underestimate the power of significant others in the client's life.

TO FORGIVE AND MOVE ON

We remarked to Freeman that he seemed very forgiving of himself and the mistakes that he had made. Maybe we noticed that because that had been a particular challenge in our own lives. "I feel bad for the kid because I think he suffered as a result of my misjudgment," he said. At the same time, what I have seen over the last 36 years of clinical practice is that things happen outside of therapy that can't be controlled by the therapist."

"I can't be angry with the mother," Freeman said, returning to the first case. "She was who she was. I can't be angry with myself either because I did what I thought best at the time. I was, however, blinded by my own 'therapeutic narcissism.' No matter how old or how experienced I get, I've got to remember that I'm a fallible human being."

We asked him to elaborate further on his therapeutic narcissism and how that got in the way. "I think this particular example made it clear enough to me that when working with adolescents I should bend over backwards to get more voice from the parents. So what I have learned from that is not be so taken with myself that I think I am that powerful, there are other people that are more powerful than me and they were there before I was on the scene."

This reminded Art about another case he dealt with recently. This was a 42-year-old man who lived with his mother. He had just made a serious attempt to kill himself. He came for the therapy session with his mother. "When I invited him into the office, his mother stood and started walking into the office. I decided at that point not to keep the mother out. I decided to have a joint interview. Having interviewed both the man and his mother together for about two thirds of the session, I then asked the man to step out of the room so I could speak with the mother."

"I am really concerned about your son," I told her. "He has made it clear that he doesn't want to come here and I'm concerned if he doesn't get some help he may be successful in killing himself next time. I need your help. I need you to be my cotherapist."

"Doctor," she answered, "I'll make sure that he will be here." Using this one-down position to recruit her help, Freeman considered that he was able to do this far more willingly now because of mistakes he had made in the past. He still felt some regret that he didn't take this position in the first case.

WHAT IS TO BE LEARNED?

We asked Freeman what others could learn from this story. "We are not as smart as we think we are. No matter how many years we have been doing therapy, and no matter how sensitive we are to our own therapeutic narcissism, we still do things that may not help, and even may hurt." Freeman paused for a moment, musing about the many manifestations of therapeutic narcissism. This was a subject about which he had been doing a fair bit of thinking over the years so it was dear to his heart. It was also a subject that ignited his passion.

"Let's take the technique of interpretation. What makes us so smart that we think we know what our clients are thinking? Certainly from a cognitive–behavior therapy perspective, it's why we use the Socratic dialogue. We don't say to a client, 'You seem angry,' but instead say, 'There is a look on your face. What does it mean? How would you put that into words?' Because indeed the client may not be angry at all, but may be pissed off, which to him or her is very different.

"Therapists love to interpret because it makes us feel as if we are really doing something useful. I don't like to use it for that reason because it really does stem from the therapeutic narcissism that says, 'I know what you are thinking.' Then, if the client says, 'No, that's not it,' we then label it *resistance.*"

A LIST OF THERAPEUTIC NARCISSISM

As a parting gift, Freeman dug deep into the files of his computer and pulled out a list he had constructed that signaled evidence of the therapist's narcissism:

1. We think we are smarter than we are.
2. We think we are more skilled than we really are.
3. We think that charisma is an adequate substitute for skill.
4. A strong theoretical grounding is unnecessary. That you don't have to learn any theory, you can take a little bit of this and a little bit of that.
5. Interpretations to the patient must be totally accepted by the patient or they are labeled as *resistant.*
6. One's theoretical model cannot or should not ever be challenged.
7. The model must be accepted as applicable to all patients without question or modification.
8. Calls for empirical support of what we do should be resisted as unnecessary.
9. Therapists believe themselves to have some sort of shamanistic function.
10. Whatever therapy we practice is the only true religion.

11. Technical approaches are to be avoided in favor of the intrinsic beauty of purely theoretical models.
12. Long-term therapy is the only "real" type of therapy.

On that note, we ended the discussion with the implication that therapeutic narcissism is at the heart of so much bad therapy. It is overconfidence, arrogance, and thinking that we know what is best for others that gets us in trouble more often than not.

Chapter 17

JOHN C. NORCROSS
50 Minutes of Pure Hostility

JOHN C. NORCROSS is known primarily for three contributions to
the field. First has been his creation of several definitive reference
books for practitioners including *Authoritative Guide to Self-Help
Resources in Mental Health*, *Insider's Guide to Graduate Programs
in Clinical and Counseling Psychology*, and *Psychologists' Desk
Reference*. Second, he has been the leading voice in the integrative
therapy movement. In his books, *Psychotherapy Relationships That
Work* and *Handbook of Psychotherapy Integration*, Norcross has
been very influential in his call for combining the best, empirically
based features of therapeutic practice into a synthesized model that
is responsive to individual and cultural differences. Finally, Norcross
has had a long-standing interest in researching and writing about
what best promotes lasting behavioral change. In his book, *Changing For Good*, he and several colleagues reached a wider audience
for their decades of research about what works best in self-initiated
change efforts.

Norcross is a professor of psychology at the University of
Scranton, Pennsylvania and a psychologist in part-time practice in
the Northern Pocono Mountains in Pennsylvania.

THE WORST I'VE EVER SEEN

Norcross is active in the American Psychological Association, both as an
officer and as a researcher. His strong roots in psychology as a profession, and empirical science as an orientation, come through quite clearly
in the way he speaks about his work. When we asked him what he had
been thinking about in anticipation of our discussion about bad therapy,
he had done his homework by preparing responses to the questions we

sent him ahead of time. For someone as organized and responsible as John, we were challenged to bring in other questions that had not been anticipated, hoping to elicit some spontaneous responses. We were not disappointed as he was most willing to talk about his failures in a very open way.

When asked how he would define bad therapy, Norcross succinctly answered that it was any treatment that did not lead to reaching declared goals or that exacerbated the client's problems. This could lead to client deterioration or perhaps premature termination.

"What is an example of that in your work?" we asked him, quickly getting to the main point of our investigation.

After hesitating a moment, trying to figure out a way to disguise the identity of the participants because of ethical concerns, John began by telling us that years ago he had been invited to serve as an expert witness on a highly visible case that had received a lot of national publicity. Although he was reluctant to take on forensic assignments, he had agreed to testify because this was one of the worst bungled cases he'd ever encountered.

"The patient suffered from major depression, and by most accounts, a narcissistic personality disorder. He had consulted a well-known psychoanalytic therapist who had begun outpatient psychotherapy with very little results. The patient had requested on multiple occasions—and these were documented in the therapist's notes—a consultation for antidepressant medication. The therapist expressed to the patient, and wrote in his notes, that he had interpreted these requests as a form of narcissistic pleading and avoiding the difficult work of therapy. Meanwhile, the patient was deteriorating and experiencing vegetative symptoms. He had to close his practice and actually went into the hospital."

This is the kind of situation that Norcross considers most inexcusable—a clinician who is so vested in his theoretical orientation, so committed to his own agenda, that he is unable to see the client's unique needs and respond to them appropriately. By interpreting the request for medication as a way to avoid the hard work of therapy, the clinician failed to consider the possibility that an alternative form of therapy may have been indicated.

Sure enough, once the patient was put on antidepressant medication, he responded well. Enraged by the way his needs had been ignored, the client sued the therapist for breech of practice standards. The case was settled out of court in favor of the client.

What bothered John most about the way this person had been treated was that the therapist refused to alter his treatment strategy, even after many months of deterioration. Even though the client had not been responding to therapy alone, at least as it had been offered, and had repeatedly asked to be reviewed for medication, the therapist refused to alter or adapt his methods. He repeatedly insisted that this was part of the resistance and that the client must continue with the original plan. We asked Norcross why he mentioned this case as the worst example of bad therapy he had ever seen. "Simple," he answered. "The patient's health was trumped by the therapist's theory."

SHAME AND HUMILITY

Moving the conversation to a discussion of his own professional experiences, we asked John how he had been feeling in anticipation of bringing up his worst case. This was not one of the questions he had anticipated, but we were curious about how he processed this internally. He struck us as so unflappable that we wondered what it was like to be him on the inside.

"So," we asked, "in reviewing your long and distinguished career, how did you decide on which case you would talk about? Talk about what this process was like for you."

"The process brought on equal parts of awareness, shame, and humility. I thought through some of the cases that might be characterized as bad sessions. There was a roar of emotions that I felt within moments of first reading the questions you would ask. I immediately said it has to be Mad Max. There was still unresolved pain and shame that led me to select this one." Not only *was*, but obviously there still *is* a lot of pain associated with this case. We prompted him to talk about the situation.

"Mad Max—of course, that is not his real name—was around 50 and recently divorced. He was court mandated to receive psychotherapy as a condition of his divorce." That's relatively rare, we thought, so asked him how that happened.

"This man was so hostile and narcissistic that the judge would not allow him to have visitation rights with his own children until he shaped up. Now the interesting thing is that he had seen a few other therapists and then he was referred to me by one of my office associates. In a single session, my colleague reported that Mad Max demeaned her as a woman and as a master's level psychiatric nurse. He insisted on seeing a real doctor."

With time to reflect on matters, John could now see that he probably should not have taken this case that was dumped on him by a colleague. Maybe he felt this would be a worthy challenge, or perhaps he felt the need to help out his colleague in distress, but one thing was for sure: his instincts told him to say no and yet he still agreed to meet with the guy. This was in spite of the fact that he already had a full caseload.

Even if he wanted to add someone else to his already overloaded schedule, this would have been the last fellow he would have considered.

"It began poorly," Norcross said. "I was angry both at the patient for mistreating my cherished colleague and at myself for accepting another referral that I didn't want or need. We had one and only one session. It was 50 minutes of pure hostility. At the beginning, the resentment and anger largely belonged to him, but toward the end the feelings were reciprocal.

"He started out by demanding what I was going to do for him. He protested that he shouldn't be here and that it was his crazy wife who had the problem. Within minutes it was clear—though he begrudgingly provided only minimal history—that his similarly self-centered and acrimonious style was exhibited toward his wife and children and his colleagues."

While trying to gather basic background information, Norcross learned that Mad Max had already seen three previous therapists, each of whom had been dismissed after a single session. Norcross could easily see why this was the case. When he discovered the man had a past history of substance abuse and tried to explore this further, he was told that this was not relevant and that Max would not speak about it.

"I tried to reflect what a difficult process this was for Max and how he felt cheated in his divorce and coerced into attending therapy. I offered several well-intended process comments about his anger. I happened to use the unfortunate term *interpersonal enactment* to describe his behavior and I could see he did not like that at all."

"What the hell kind of psychobabble is that?" Mad Max challenged him. Realizing his error, Norcross quickly apologized. He admitted this was a poor word choice and thanked Max for catching it. "Well, all right," Mad Max conceded grudgingly. "But don't do it again!"

"That was the straw that broke the camel's back in terms of my hostility," John admits. "At that point, I engaged in some pejorative interpretations which, even as I speak about it now, I feel ashamed. Surely I know better. Although his narcissism and anger were masking his depression and insecurity, nonetheless I was brought right into it."

Using as much restraint as he could muster, Norcross explained to Mad Max that therapy required a degree of commitment that was lacking in this case. He said mildly, "This seems to be getting in the way of our work together."

"Oh, so now you're blaming me?" Mad Max challenged him. "You think this is all my fault?"

"No," Norcross responded. "I'm blaming the process and wondering how we can make it different."

"That's what you say but you're really implying that it's all me."

At this point, Norcross was thinking to himself, "Well, if the shoe fits, wear it." In fact, he said something similar: "In this session, it does appear that you have a major role in blocking our work. I am trying to sustain a relationship with you, but when someone is insulting me and demanding and snapping at me I find that difficult. I'm prepared to like you, and I'm really trying." With this disclosure and confrontation, Norcross was hoping that he might break through to the man. He was not so lucky.

"Look," Mad Max said, seeming to become more enraged when Norcross apologized. "Don't be so soft. Don't be gay."

"I find that comment very offensive," John replied testily. He had rarely felt so frustrated and blocked with a client in his life and yet he couldn't get a handle on what he could do to take things to a different level. Norcross was reluctant to get in much detail about how the session further deteriorated. "Let's just say he made an extraordinarily vicious comment about anyone gay or lesbian, and I didn't appreciate it. We ended by saying this was a difficult session, and I immediately praised his honesty for letting things out. Max said that since the judge told him that he had to attend therapy he would make an appointment. When he called a few days later to cancel the appointment, I did not protest."

UPON REFLECTION

As Norcross looked back on this session he felt genuinely regretful about the way he had handled it. He realized now that things were doomed from the start.

"There were unresolved resentments toward my colleague, toward my patient, and toward myself for even seeing this man in the first place. As I mentioned, it is painful to recall that after all these years I would have been caught up in his provocative and hostile demeanor. It was a beginner's mistake: not monitoring my countertransference better. When I did try to recognize Max's pain, though it was well-intended, I put it in a way that he experienced as feminine or homosexual in orientation. I should have noted that earlier and found a different way of reaching him."

Although this incident had occurred five years earlier, it was still painful for John to talk about. We wonder about how this excruciating lesson impacted him, how it changed the way he operated in the future.

"There is an interesting twist to this. Two years ago, I got a call out of the blue from Mad Max. He said he had been through several more therapists. *Through* was his word—though I think that is probably an apt description. He said that he had met the minimum criteria for the court ordered psychotherapy but that he hadn't improved worth a damn. Those were his words—not a damn."

"I'm sorry to hear that," Norcross responded cautiously. "How would you like things to change?"

"Look," Mad Max said. "I know I am an angry, self-centered guy. I know I'm alienating people right and left. But I really would like to change."

"Why, may I ask, are you calling me now?" What Norcross wanted to say, but didn't, was why the hell Max was calling him if their first session had been so awful. But Norcross had had plenty of time to reflect on matters since then and he resolved that if he ever talked with the guy again he would do so calmly and professionally.

"Well, the rest of the therapists either just yelled at me from the word go or just sat there and nodded their heads and said, 'Uh, huh.' I respected you because at least you were honest with me. I know I gave you a hard time," he added. It turned out that Mad Max had since moved from the area and was calling for a referral of someone else who lived nearby. Norcross agonized for a minute or two about whom he knew that he could refer this guy to. We kidded that it would have to be a colleague he didn't like very much.

"Yeah," Norcross laughed, "or someone who owed me a big favor."

THE CLIENT PRIMARILY DETERMINES THE OUTCOME

Norcross takes some consolation that although he considers this his worst session, the client seemed to gain something useful from the experience. That is one of the most peculiar things about studying our subject: Sometimes the client and therapist have very different judgments about what is good and bad therapy. Or sometimes what looks like bad therapy in the short-run turns out to have a good outcome in the long run.

Since the case that Norcross brought up illustrated a time when he considered it his worst work, yet the client considered it somewhat helpful in retrospect, we wondered if he could think of an instance in which the opposite occurred: he had done good work but the client considered it lousy.

"I don't have any of those experiences, largely because I define the success of the session in terms of the patient's appraisal. A good part of my therapy in virtually every session is to monitor the patient's response and reactions to what is occurring. So, there are certainly those times when we are approaching the end of the session that I think it went reasonably well, or that I offered a presence or a method or an awareness that may have helped the patient. But when I asked the patient how the session was, or what we should do in subsequent sessions, the patient was not nearly as positive as I was. Then I immediately reevaluate my perception of the success of that particular session."

Norcross supported his point with some empirical research conducted by several colleagues that consistently finds that therapists are often not particularly good judges of the therapy outcomes and patient appraisals. He considered it far more useful to use the client's perception, which is why he monitors those reactions so carefully. He said that he was especially careful to do so in the early stages of the relationship when the client would be less inclined to be forthcoming about negative reactions. "But as therapy evolves, I find patients are not only willing but downright eager to have some input into the direction of their therapy."

We asked him how he handled the negative feedback when things were not going well. We recalled our own most recent instances when students or clients told us they didn't like what we were doing and how we were doing it.

"It's a slight narcissistic wound," John admitted, "but over the years I have reaped the benefits of patients tailoring me to their own needs. So, in the long run, I certainly can tolerate some discomfort or disagreement for their long-term benefit." We prompted him to say more about that.

"Toward the end of most sessions I summarize what has occurred in the session, perhaps reviewing some between-session goals or tasks they would like to accomplish. I ask patients how the session was for them that day. My question is purposely open-ended so that patients can talk about their internal experiences, my contributions, and the content. They answer in all sorts of different ways. They will say they were surprised where it went, or that they were disappointed, or they weren't aware of something in particular. I'll follow up on this, asking them how this experience guides what we might do next.

"I have found that both the content and the process of the patient's answer are incredibly rich, both in terms of their therapy and how I can customize or individualize the experience next time."

The answer to this question gives Norcross a cue as to when they should schedule the next appointment. Interestingly, he doesn't see most of his clients every week. Again, he cites research, as well as his own experience, that indicates that except in the case of crisis, weekly sessions are not necessarily more helpful than meeting every second or third week. Instead of saying to a client, "What time next week?" he asks, "When would you like to schedule the next appointment?"

WHAT COULD OTHERS LEARN?

The final area we wanted to explore with Norcross was his opinion about what therapists could do to learn more from their failures. How could others extrapolate from his experience?

"I think I can answer that in two ways. One is the lesson that I have learned and then have extended to others. In that way, my personal experiences seem to be training lessons. When I reflect on Mad Max, and my contributions to the conflict, I have learned—or more accurately re-learned—several fundamental lessons. First, we need to set and maintain boundaries on referrals. It's disappointing when I realize that self-care is more of a research area than a personal competency for me. That is some of the shame I feel. And that is why when people read some of my self-care articles they assume that somehow I have mastered this. I immediately say that my self-care research is transparent compensation. I am researching and writing on it hoping that I get it.

"Second, I need to be more aware of ubiquitous countertransference. I should have processed part of this with my colleague and myself before seeing the patient.

"Third, I've learned both from Mad Max, and from research, that strongly resistant or oppositional patients require a form of psychotherapy and a therapist stance that is quite different from most patients. It should involve low therapist directiveness, emphasizing client self-control procedures. I didn't do that well early on.

"The other part of this is what trainees might learn. A significant benefit of seasoned therapists acknowledging bad sessions might be the realization that virtually all of us have similar sessions. But due to confidentiality, or isolation, most of us overpersonalize our own failures, when in reality they seem to be part and parcel of our common world."

John's words reminded us both that because therapists so rarely and openly talk about bad therapy, we think we are the only ones doing it. So, we asked him in what ways his colleagues tended to overpersonalize their failures.

"I conduct a lot of psychotherapy supervision. One of the hallmarks of a good supervisory relationship is when trainees can tell me about some of their feelings about a bad session or an improper interpretation or just something 'wrong' in the session. Immediately, when they do so, you can see the shoulders lift. The shame begins to diminish. You can just see a sudden feeling shift in the student. When I can share that I certainly have had many of these experiences myself, students no longer feel uniquely or singularly wretched. They are surprised that other people might have had these experiences because surely in most videotapes and psychotherapy textbooks we present only the good cases. We do not publicly share bad sessions or treatment failures. Appreciating the universality of the struggles of psychotherapy might lead to corrective actions in the sense that we are not alone."

As a final note, Norcross thanked us for doing this project. "If seasoned therapists can candidly acknowledge our own bad sessions, I think it might provide comfort to all. This is true particularly for trainees, also for ourselves."

Chapter 18

LEN SPERRY
Letting Things Get Personal

LEN SPERRY was trained as both a physician and a psychologist. This diverse background is reflected in his writing and clinical practice as well. In his books (many of which are collaborations with Jon Carlson), he is known for his work in spiritual aspects of counseling (*Ministry and Community, Spirituality in Clinical Practice, Transforming Self and Community: Revisioning Pastoral Counseling*); Adlerian therapy (*Counseling and Psychotherapy: An Integrated, Individual Psychology Approach, Adlerian Counseling and Therapy*); cognitive therapy (*Cognitive Behavior Therapy of DSM IV Personality Disorders*); treatment planning (*Psychopathology and Psychotherapy: From DSM-IV Diagnosis to Treatment, Handbook of Diagnosis and Treatment, Treatment Outcomes in Psychotherapy*); marital therapy (*Marital Therapy: Integrating Theory and Technique, The Disordered Couple, The Intimate Couple, Brief Therapy with Individuals and Couples*); and community health (*Health Counseling, Psychiatric Consultation in the Workplace, Aging in the 21st Century*).

Sperry is on the faculty of the Departments of Health Service Administration and Psychology at Barry University, Miami Shores, Florida.

POOR JUDGMENTS

We began our conversation with Len Sperry by defining what bad therapy meant to him. This was a subject to which he had given considerable thought, so he approached it from multiple perspectives. The first thing that occurred to him was that such a negative outcome occurred when the client was somehow diminished by the experience. Then, he thought for a second, and mentioned another possibility that we hadn't readily considered: In one sense, bad therapy takes place even if the *therapist* is diminished by the experience. In other words, the results of a partnership are assessed by the perceptions of *both* participants.

Warming to the topic, Len took a more objective viewpoint. "If a treatment has no sound basis for being used, and the client is hurt as a result of this effort, then that is definitely bad therapy." Taking things a step further, Len decided to be provocative: "I would say that when most regressive therapies are done with people who don't have very much of a cohesive self, these are bad therapies." He waited for an argument from us; when he didn't get one, he continued: "In the first case, I am being more general, that any time therapy hurts one or both people in the process it is not an effective effort. More specifically, I think there are some kinds of therapy that are particularly ill-advised, especially in situations when clients are vulnerable and not able to make informed choices about their participation."

When pressed for an example, Len immediately cited a situation of working with a brittle borderline personality disorder, or perhaps someone with an identity disorder. There are certain kinds of treatments that should absolutely not be used with these cases and others that are far more likely to produce good outcomes. There was passion in his voice when he reminded us of the dictum of all healers and helpers that, above all else, we should do no harm. Len had little patience for practitioners who use treatments that are not clinically sound or scientifically supported.

"Let's say that someone is in the midst of trauma and I'm using an exploratory, regressive therapy where we're processing very primitive dynamics, to the point where the client decompensates. These individuals might not have very good defenses and boundaries. If things go wrong, they could take a long time to recover from that sort of treatment."

Len considered what he had said, then added that with other clients who have more intact egos and more evolved defenses, perhaps these treatments could be helpful to them. But his main point was that making poor clinical judgments are what get us in trouble.

GETTING PERSONAL

Conscious of the intellectual tone of the conversation so far, we turned far more personal. When Len was asked about his own worst cases, he mentioned two that came instantly to mind, one in group therapy and the other in family therapy. Most consistently throughout his career, these are the two modalities that he finds most challenging and those that have tested him the most.

Sperry recalled a time very early in his career during his psychiatric residency when he was working with an inpatient group that met five days a week. "On this one particular day the attending psychiatrist for the inpatient unit was gone. I had been the leader of the group, sometimes working with another clinician who would act as cotherapist as she did this day. "Once the group got started, one of the patients—a male borderline—started to become fairly agitated. He did an admirable job of getting everyone else worked up and derailed from their issues." Although Len smiled at the memory, he was hardly amused by what happened next.

"I said something that must have come across to this young man as a very paternal father-figure type of statement. I should mention that he was loose enough that he experienced a psychotic transference to me. Anyway, he just became enraged. He stood up and started acting in a very threatening manner toward me."

Sperry stopped the story to explain that in such situations it was usually agreed to have an arrangement with a cotherapist to intervene in such situations so as to neutralize the transference, deflect the aggression, and get things back on track. That's what he liked most about group therapy in the first place, that the work doesn't get bogged down in a lot of transference stuff since issues become diluted by other members who are present. Even if that fails, at least there is a partner around who can help calm things down and act as a mediator

"In this situation my cotherapist seemed to be on autopilot. She just sat there sort of stunned and did nothing. I felt frozen as well. I couldn't do anything. I couldn't think what to say. Until this guy calmed down, I felt helpless. And it took a very long time for his anger to run its course."

Returning to his previous definitions of what constitutes bad therapy, Sperry was certain that this experience qualified since not only did the client have a hard time with what was going on, and in a manner that was not especially therapeutic, but also both therapists felt traumatized by the encounter. "It seemed that all my inexperience was showing. I let the client down because I didn't know how to handle the situation and how to be helpful."

Len also felt disappointed and angry with his cotherapist, who should have jumped in and smoothed things over. She was far more experienced on the unit and she was the one who was supposed to be watching over him.

"Because of our mistakes, this client, and everyone else in the group, had an experience that was far too close to the way their everyday lives were structured. They were already subjected to situations in life that were unsafe and it was our job to protect them from further abuse. We let them down."

Sperry recalled how frightened he had been by that experience, and how helpless he had felt. Usually able to respond well in most situations, no matter what the circumstances, he felt humbled as he faced his limits. Looking back on the episode, he saw it as one of his most formative training experiences.

"At this time I was seeing so many people with disorders of the self—borderline and narcissistic personality disorders. After this situation, it only heightened my interest in working with these people. So that was my adaptive response to feeling helpless."

Sperry was able to use what he learned from that episode in so many ways. It became a pattern throughout his life and career to take such setbacks and use them to redouble his efforts to handle them differently in the future. Rather than trying to avoid such tough cases in the future, he resolved to specialize in dealing effectively with psychotic transference.

IF I COULD DO IT DIFFERENTLY

Sperry was asked what he would have done differently in such a situation. Without hesitance, he listed several lessons he had learned. If he was ever going to work with someone again as a partner he would be certain they had clear expectations for one another's behavior and would cover one another's back. "One of the basic rules in cotherapy," Len said, "is when you are doing a group or family together, if one of the therapists gets pinned against the wall, or gets in trouble, it is important to offer support as needed. The cotherapist's role is to somehow redirect, to refocus, and to allow the situation to calm down so that you can process it. That allows it to be therapeutic. And, of course, you try to keep situations from escalating."

Len took full responsibility for his lack of preparation and failure to coordinate his actions with those of his partner. Yes, there was a press of time and he was thrust into the situation without much warning; nevertheless, he realized afterwards that he should have taken the time to coordinate their efforts, even if it was just a few minutes to review their respective roles. This was a mistake he would never make today.

So in this particular example of bad therapy, there was just one little step left out, a seemingly insignificant component, yet one that had vast consequences—for the client, the other group members, and the leaders. Even when Len leads a group alone now he makes certain to gather enough detail in his presession preparation about the status of each participant, reports from hospital staff, outstanding concerns that have been raised, crises that have come up, and any acute problems that are on the horizon.

A FAMILY DISASTER

Changing the subject to another case that came to mind, Sperry described a family meeting he had arranged with a patient he was seeing in individual therapy as well as managing his medication.

"This was a 73-year-old man with progressive memory problems. It had become clear that this person was having dementia of the Alzheimer's type. After three sessions together, his family wanted to meet with me so I agreed to schedule such a gathering. Well, his wife came and brought their 36-year-old, recently divorced, daughter. Before I even had a chance to get things going, the daughter jumped in right away and began saying how I wasn't treating her father well and I was doing a lousy job. She listed all the side effects he was suffering as a result of the drugs I had prescribed.

"I calmly and systematically reviewed the very standard regiment that he was on for this dementia and his anxiety symptoms. I made certain to engage the wife during this discussion because it was clear from her nonverbal behaviors that she was quite concerned about what had been happening recently. She had mentioned that her husband had gotten worse, but what became clear in a very short period of time was that, unbeknownst to me, the mother and daughter had started feeding this patient a set of herbs and herb combinations that had accounted for his side effects because they had interacted with the medication to make his behavior really bizarre.

"Not only was his memory worse, but he was delusional and agitated at the same time. When I had done the initial evaluation on the husband and I had asked the wife specifically about any kinds of over-the-counter medications or vitamins or herbal remedies and so forth, and she had denied that she was using anything. He had, in fact, been using these things all along.

"What happened here was that the wife was quite understanding about the need to reduce my medications or their substances. The daughter, on the other hand, continued to blame and attack me for my perceived incompetence. She threatened to sue me. Eventually, she sent a really nasty letter to the clinic director."

It sounded as if Sperry was relatively blameless for this fiasco but he was quick to point out that he handled things poorly. He admitted that he overreacted and became defensive rather than trying to work with the family as part of a team in which they were all doing their best to help the man.

"It wasn't until afterwards that I recognized her personality style and dynamics were very similar to mine. The failure on my part to step back from the attack at the moment and look at it from their perspective." Again, Len recognized that there were some countertransference dynamics going on, feelings that he didn't recognize or address until it was too late.

"I probably could have continued to talk with the patient, and with the patient's wife, in a very calm way. I had made a very small comment at the end of the session that demonstrated my indignation that they had not been upfront with what they were doing. It was directed at all of them, but I think they took this very personally that I was attacking them and accusing them of hurting their family member."

One of the things that Sperry demonstrated in the telling of this case was his own willingness to examine and acknowledge his mistakes. It is only from such self-reflection, and honesty, that we can ever hope to learn from these failures.

Chapter 19

SCOTT D. MILLER
I Should Have Known Better

SCOTT MILLER has been working with a team of coresearchers for the past 10 years to develop reliable, empirically supported principles for psychotherapy practice. In his book, *The Heart and Soul of Change*, he and colleagues Mark Hubble and Barry Duncan brought together much of what is currently known about "what works" in therapy into a single volume that informs practitioners about effective treatment. In a series of other books such as *The Heroic Client, Escape From Babel*, and *Psychotherapy with Impossible Cases* the team of coworkers talk about the crucial role that clients play in their own treatments. Scott has also written extensively about solution-focused therapy in several books, *Handbook of Solution-Focused Brief Therapy, The Miracle Method*, and *Working with the Problem Drinker*. The hallmark of his writing and teaching voice is a blending of scientific thinking with a gentle sensitivity to human experience.

Miller has applied what he has learned from his research and practice to real-world social problems. For a number of years he codirected a clinic specializing in providing services to homeless people. He continues to devote a portion of his time to working with disadvantaged and underserved populations.

In this discussion on failures in therapy, Scott applied his keen intellect and systematic thinking to sort out the different kinds of therapeutic failures that can occur and how they may be differentially identified.

DRIVEN BY FAILURES

We were initially interested in what Miller had been thinking about while preparing for this conversation. We expected that he would organize his remarks with the same efficiency with which he approaches other facets of his work. We were not disappointed.

"I had a series of posttraumatic memories thinking about some of my cases," Scott reveals without preamble. "This wasn't because I thought the cases weren't going well so much as the clients didn't believe they were going well, and they got mad about it."

Miller further remarked that things are so much easier to handle when clients just go away when they are unhappy with progress rather than those who return to remind the therapist of their dissatisfaction. He admitted that he has had a few of these clients in his career and the memories of them still plague him.

"Those were the initial thoughts I had about the subject, but then the more I actually started to think about it, I realized how much in my therapeutic style has probably been driven by failures—that is, failures in my individual work with clients, as well as failures in how I think about therapy, my theories." As he now understands the development of his ideas and methods, mistakes, missteps, and miscalculations helped Scott more than anything else to get better at what he does.

FAILURES VERSUS NOT-SUCCESSES

We knew from having read Miller's books and seeing him work on demonstration videos that he was likely to have a rather precise definition of what failure meant to him. When we asked him how he thought about what constitutes failure in therapy, he identified two distinct kinds.

"One is where any improvement while in therapy is not necessarily a result of the therapy. I would consider that a failure. A large percentage of clients seem to get better on their own, in spite of me, or in spite of other therapists. I would consider that by definition a failure because the therapy didn't add anything to what would have happened either by chance, by error, maturation of the person, or by the passage of time." We asked Scott to elaborate further on the research terms he favored.

"Well, there is all sorts of random variance, error variance, that enters into the equation when you are trying to analyze change. A failure for me is when the amount of variance attributable to such factors is not distinguishable from that contributed by the therapy. So you have to say it was a failure. I call it a 'not success.' This is not so much a failure but a case of not success."

Confused by this distinction, we asked him to provide an example of what he meant. "I routinely administer an outcome measure to my clients that has what's called a Reliable Change Index. Simply put, 'reliable change' is the amount of change that is greater than error, greater than the passage of time, and greater than the maturation of the client. If the amount of change a client experiences while in therapy is not greater than that amount—the Reliable Change Index—then that is a 'not success.' I can't attribute the change to my work with the client."

We made quick mental adjustments in our heads as we listened to Miller speak. Entering the world of each master therapist requires us to hear and use different language systems. Although each of our contributors may be doing very similar things with their clients, they certainly talk about the process in different ways. In Miller's case, much of the way he understands and talks about therapy is quite consistent with the research processes he employs to find answers to questions that interest him.

So then, we asked him to simplify a bit. He said quite succinctly that therapists develop ideas about what works in therapy when the client may very well have improved anyway, not as a function of any intervention. Okay, so that's one kind of failure in therapy that he calls "not success." What, then, of the other kind?

"That is when clients 'reliably' deteriorate in my presence. They get worse in the context of my relationship, more than what would have happened by chance alone. Those are the ones that I would describe as real failures. Something I did, or didn't do, ended up making the client worse."

POSTTRAUMATIC MEMORIES

Hoping that we could delve more deeply into the more serious lapses—failures rather than not-successes—we asked Scott how he settled on the particular case that he wanted to tell us about. We wondered what the process was like for him in making his selection among the possibilities.

"The clients that I think most about have been reliable failures. These are cases that once in a while, for whatever reason—either a certain smell, a certain look on the face of a client—bring back a host of memories. Or maybe I'll be walking down the street and I'll see somebody who reminds me of this particular client. When this happens I am reminded of the client, I can almost hear them calling out to me: 'Hey, why aren't you helping me?' Or worse yet: 'Your help is making me worse.'" We asked Miller which of these posttraumatic memories haunted him the most?

"This was a woman in her mid-30s. She had a history of polysubstance abuse. She came to me reporting that she had been to see another therapist who'd ended up having sex with her. Of course, she felt hurt and traumatized by this. She had heard about me either by reading one of my articles or seeing a book that I had written or some interview that I had done."

Miller began the treatment by scheduling weekly appointments, which were later changed to more frequent sessions after more traumatic material emerged. It turned out that in addition to being sexually abused by her previous therapist, she had been abused by her father when she was younger. As if this wasn't enough to deal with, her mother was an active alcoholic who was quite emotionally abusive toward her.

Miller explained that he was following his usual regimen of strength-based interventions, when we asked him to give some background on how he works for those unfamiliar with his approach.

"I try to see what clients bring into the room with them, their background, their culture, their language, their abilities, their support network, their ideas about how change happens, the strengths that I can use and capitalize on in trying to help them. I do this rather than identifying deficits that I somehow need to fix. I see clients as the authors of therapy sessions and I see my role as the witness, or the audience, applauding at the appropriate times.

"The more we talked together, the more complicated the story became, and the more material came up. At the same time, much of what she had complained about initially—chronic feelings of emptiness and depression, sadness, difficult interpersonal relationships, risky sexual and other personal behavior like taking drugs—didn't really change. I understood her idea about the change process to be that we needed to get to the core of what it was that was bothering her, to the root of this thing and address those roots. We continued to do that but no meaningful changes in those complaints occurred."

We were struck by the eclectic nature of Miller's conceptual framework. He utilized empirically based scientific language, favored a solution-focused model, borrowed ideas from narrative and other constructionist frameworks, and yet also talked about getting to the roots of the problem in a way that would be familiar to a psychodynamic practitioner. We wondered what Scott was thinking about all this when he observed that in spite of his best efforts to be helpful, the client continued to deteriorate.

"I was thinking, first of all, that I couldn't apply my old ideas to this particular person. I couldn't use my traditional way of thinking and experience. I had to follow the client's directive to a tee. That was my first thought." We noticed that he had adopted a strategic approach of paying attention to what wasn't working, abandoning that, and trying something else. We also noticed that one of the hallmarks of his approach emerged again—the care and sensitivity with which he offers to let the client lead the process.

TIME TO GET SOME HELP

After noticing, and then accepting, that what he was doing was not working, Miller's second thought was that he had better reach out to colleagues for support, consultation, and supervision. He discussed the case
with two different supervisors.

"One person, whom I chose purposely, came from a psychodynamic
orientation. I did this since the client I was seeing seemed to be of that
bent herself. This supervisor's own theory was about getting to the core
of the issue, discovering what had really happened, addressing that, and
restoring some sense of personal boundaries. The other supervisor was
oriented much more as a strategic family therapist. The first psychodynamic supervisor said to me that this client was exhibiting all the signs of
borderline personality disorder and that I needed to set appropriate boundaries and begin to gently confront some of the issues she was presenting.
On the other hand, the family therapist said that I needed to stay the
course, continue to highlight strengths and resources, and perhaps introduce some narrative ideas because of the ways she conceived of the original trauma. So maybe I should externalize all of this angst and trauma
and talk about how the client was going to 'stand up' to that trauma
instead of allowing it to engulf and swallow her."

We felt uneasy, vicariously, listening to Scott telling the story of trying to find some help for his confusion. As if this business isn't tough
enough, when we do confront challenging cases, our consultations often
make things worse rather than better. It is entirely possible that we could
ask half a dozen supervisors what to do with a case and get a different
answer from each one. All we are left with is the realization that there are
so many more options than we had originally considered, but still no
consensus as to best practices. So, then we asked Miller what happened
next after he talked to his colleagues for advice. "Nothing. Not a damned
thing happened. And at this point I had been seeing the client for close to
2 years. This is *very* unusual for me. After all, I've made a name for
myself as a *brief* therapist.

MAKING SENSE OF WHAT WENT WRONG

So far, it sounded to us as if Miller had handled things entirely appropriately. We wondered what he thought he had done wrong. The first thing
he mentioned was that once he realized that what he had been doing
wasn't working, he should have tried something completely different.

Surely 2 years was an awfully long time to keep doing basically the same things.

When he reviewed his conduct, Scott admitted that he handled things just the way he would today. He maintained professional boundaries. He made himself available to the client as much as was reasonable. "She was never a person who called me on the phone," Miller said, "that is, until I moved to end the therapy. Then suddenly the phone calls and escalation began."

Before we got into what led to the exacerbation of problems, we asked Miller again about how he failed this client. In truth, we were each reliving our own traumatic memories of similar clients who manifested manipulative, borderline-type qualities and didn't get significantly better in spite of our most noble, concerted efforts. In reviewing our own such cases, we acknowledged that most of the time when we got into trouble (and still do) was when we were trying too hard, or when we overpersonalized what was going on. Miller's answer, however, surprised us. In retrospect, he considered this a case that was outside his area of expertise. "I went beyond what I knew how to do."

AND THEN WHAT HAPPENED?

Going back to the story, we were hungry to hear what happened next and how things turned out. After 2 years of weekly sessions, or sometimes twice weekly appointments, there had been no appreciable change in her behavior or her complaints. The only consolation was that the two of them enjoyed a great relationship and a strong alliance. Scott knew this was the case because he made an effort to use a standardized alliance measure periodically to see how things were progressing.

Eventually, Miller just gave up, realizing that he probably could not help her. Although he thought he was trying to offer her a better alternative, she experienced the suggestion as a personal rejection, a repudiation of the trust that she had felt toward him. It was another betrayal in her mind.

Being brutally honest with himself about his limitations, Miller admitted that with this particular case he was in over his head. We both nodded our heads, not in agreement but in commiseration, thinking about people we were seeing who tested us beyond what we felt competent to handle. But in one way that is what is so wonderful about this work we do—no matter how long we do it, we will never, ever get it right.

And then we prompted Scott to continue the narrative. "She stormed out of the office that day. The more I tried to explain what I was thinking about, the more she took it as both a personal criticism and abandonment. I called her on the phone and invited her to return so we could figure out a way to end things. She said she wanted to continue. I told her that it didn't make a lot of sense to me to continue with something that wasn't being very helpful."

Finally, the woman did return to try and work things out. Or at least that is what she said. In the meantime, she had begun to act more self-destructively. She had anonymous sexual encounters with men she met at bars. She also began to use drugs again.

"I told her that I felt terrible about that. We should try to see what we could do to bridge this breech in the alliance while simultaneously trying to communicate that I didn't believe further, more of the same ineffective stuff was going to result in anything different.

"If you do an autopsy of this, there are probably lots of reasons that took place that are congruent with this client's experience in life. She felt rejected by her parents and abused in the relationship so she was probably pretty sensitive to this stuff. But I don't see that as an excuse for what transpired. I think if I had suggested this *earlier* then maybe we would not have experienced this and she would have seen that as an expression of concern rather than abandonment."

SOME REGRETS

Miller had started talking in the beginning about the posttraumatic memories that still haunted him. At times he would see or hear someone who reminded him of this woman and he would feel flooded with regrets about how he handled things. We wondered what has been hardest for him in processing this experience.

"If I am completely honest with you, there are two pieces that are hard. One of them is that I hate not succeeding. I hate it when people leave and feel dissatisfied with me. That plays into all my own personal issues and probably one of the reasons I became a therapist."

Now *that* struck a resonant chord. So much of Jeffrey's own writing had been about the personal motives that lead us to this profession, how our feelings of inadequacy, our fears of failure, our unresolved issues, our search for approval and validation, our hunger for intimacy, our search for personal meaning, led us to do this difficult job. Whether it was a benefit and privilege of being a therapist, or rather a side effect and scourge, it is indeed difficult to escape the ways our personal issues are triggered by our clients. If he was willing, we invited Scott to say more about how his personal history entered into this situation. "In my family, I was a middle child and I think that sort of led me to be the entertainer. I didn't have the status of the first son; neither was I the baby of the family; I was right smack dab in the middle. I was, therefore, undistinguished in any important respect. So I think that trying to please people, to be funny and humorous, to be clever and helpful was sort of the role that I distinguished for myself. Not doing that feels awful to me, but equally awful was when I ended up with phone calls from this client saying what a schmuck I was and she was going to 'tell on me.'"

In other words, Miller had failed her, and himself. "So I was both fearful and then frightened about what had happened. In the midst of this I felt exposed because this person then contacted a colleague of mine, a well-known therapist, who got involved in this case. The client was flying out to see this therapist who was then advising her both about what I was doing wrong and also offering to supervise me."

Still angry about the way this was handled, especially at a time when both he and his client were so vulnerable, Scott explained that he had sought supervision almost a year earlier. "I felt there was a surprising kind of blindness on the part of this colleague—whose work I actually respected up to this point—about the complicated nature of this relationship. I couldn't talk to this colleague though because I had no legal right to do that. So I couldn't call this person on the phone and say, 'Hey, let me tell you what is going on. Let me give you a full picture.'"

At this point, the failed therapy not only ended up in the open for another to see but it ended up triangulated. Miller couldn't remain involved any longer in the case and so stood helplessly aside as this new therapist offered to come to the rescue.

ATTENTIVE TO PATTERNS

Now to the bottom line: we asked Miller what he learned from all this. "Never to see clients again." We laughed appreciatively.

"I learned that I needed to be attentive to patterns of nonsuccess and failure. I needed to be more sensitive to knowing at what point my knowledge, or my ability, or my connection with the client, was not likely to lead to any better results. That led me to this whole business of measuring outcomes and trying to use outcome scores to predict the likely trajectory of change of clients in an individual therapeutic relationship with me."

It was interesting that a failure like this was so seminal in Miller's development as a researcher and a practitioner. This particular case had a strong influence in pushing him to be more precise in measuring and predicting the effects of his interventions. What can others learn from this?

"I was just outside working in the yard. I was picking up dog poop, which I hate to do. But if I didn't have to pick up the dog poop, then I wouldn't have this dog that I love. I guess I'm trying to say that I don't think that having failures is the problem per se. But to allow a failure to continue over a long period of time, much beyond where you are usually successful with people, that is troubling."

So one theme that emerged from this was about knowing your limits and being brutally honest with yourself when you are not having the effects you want. We were still trying to make the connection to the dog poop metaphor, when Miller continued in a soft voice, "I should have known better. I am the person who is running around the country saying that techniques contribute a paltry 15% of the outcome of therapy. And yet everything that I tried to do was along those lines. I don't know what I was thinking except that I really wanted to help this particular person and I really liked her and felt moved by her story. I think the main thing to take away is that my doggedness and my reliance on techniques were not enough, could never have been enough. I should have seen this earlier and made my failure a success by helping connect this client to something or someone else."

FOLLOW-UP

We returned to the story and wondered if there was any further resolution, or at least contact.

"Well, I never talked with the third party [the meddling therapist]. The client wanted to see me and the other therapist concurrently. The supervision I was getting from the psychodynamic person suggested that this particular way of working wasn't in the best interest of the client. In fact, this was part of a pattern of triangulating people in her life. Now whether or not that was true I don't know, but I was feeling confused. Following through with this advice did not endear me to either the client or her new therapist though. In fact, I later learned that the other therapist wrote about this case, calling me an 'asshole' in print! That was another painful thing about this case. Two colleagues were amazingly supportive, both toward me and the client, during this very difficult time. But I also found that this other therapist was very willing to move in and rescue and then somehow glorify himself on the hill of my failure. This was disturbing and hurtful. It's pretty much soured my relationship with that particular person."

We told Scott, quite sincerely, that it took a lot of courage to do what he was doing right now with us. He was willing to talk about this failure so openly, and yet talk about his own resilience. We wondered what allowed him to keep going forward, to be willing to be so honest and talk about this failure when be got burned before by being open and vulnerable.

"I guess the bottom line is that this client didn't do anything to me. I think it restores my faith in the idea that the client is the director and I am sort of the witness. Since nothing bad happened to me, my fundamental tenets about humanity weren't shaken to the core. I never ever believed that is what this person wanted. I always thought that what she wanted was to feel okay and to be all right and not be tortured by memories of her past. That's what I wanted for her too. This was confirmed when we exchanged a couple of e-mails and a phone call a couple of years later. So, I feel that my fundamental experience of this person was accurate, I personally was just not able to be of help to her the way I would have liked, and I wish I had been aware of that earlier. "

How should other therapists process their own nonsuccesses and failures? How would Miller advise other therapists to process their own nonsuccesses and reliable failures?

"You have to be able to distinguish between the two. I think a lot of what passes for wisdom in our field about both success and failure is random or chance variations in outcome. I think that is why we have 400 different treatment models since everyone can say something about psychotherapy and it's true at some time."

Chapter 20

MICHAEL F. HOYT
I Was Blind at the Time

Based at the Kaiser Permanente Medical Center, San Rafael, California and at the University of California School of Medicine, San Francisco, MICHAEL F. HOYT is one of the leading voices in the brief therapy movement. Since the early 1990s, he has specialized in writing and teaching about ways that therapy may be practiced more efficiently, effectively, and with concern for available time and resources. Many of his ideas have been published in *Brief Therapy and Managed Care, Constructive Therapies, The Handbook of Constructive Therapies, The First Session in Brief Therapy, Some Stories Are Better Than Others,* and *Interviews with Brief Therapy Experts.*

A BAD TASTE IN MY MOUTH

Michael told us that he had been warned by some colleagues to be cautious about participating in this project. "After all," they said, "you won't want people to think you do bad therapy." This kind of attitude continues to perplex us, as it did Hoyt—that people in our field really believe that we shouldn't even talk about our mistakes and failures, much less ever admit that we engage in less than perfect work. Hoyt explained that he was open to discussing his "bad therapy" if doing so might create opportunities for him and others to learn from the errors.

Hoyt defined bad therapy simply as "that which is injurious or harmful or that fails through incompetence or is way below standard performance. Something that was morally evil or unethical would also be bad, of course. What you did was very clumsy, or wrong, or funky, or stupid. It's when you go 'Ewww!' You think to yourself that you should not have done that, that you should have known better. For me, bad therapy is different from therapy that just wasn't good or helpful—it leaves a bad taste in one's mouth."

Never one to pass up the opportunity to be playful, Jon asked exactly what bad therapy tastes like. Michael was about to answer before he realized that Jon was kidding. But then he considered the question seriously for a moment. "For me, it's a sour taste," he said. "It's something repugnant. When it happens, you go 'Yuck,' and you shake your head."

We noticed that in the conversation that followed, Hoyt was distancing himself a bit from the subject, sometimes even using the pronouns *you* and *they* rather than *I* to talk about examples of bad therapy. We wondered if that was because of the tendency that many of us have to be harsher critics of other people's mistakes than our own. Hoyt agreed.

"When I look back and say I did bad therapy I certainly wasn't trying to do bad therapy. I was blind at the time. I was out of control or anxious or confused. I was not malevolent. I didn't have a nasty intention in any way.

"Yet when I am watching someone else, or I am supervising or watching a tape, and it looks really bad I'll be more moralistic and judgmental toward the person. I'll say that 'He shouldn't have done that' and 'She ought to know better than that.' You're right; I can be pretty hard on myself, too, but sometimes it's easier to be harsh to 'them' and less harsh to 'me.'"

We thought about that for a moment. During the silence, while Jon prepared the next place to lead the conversation, Jeffrey noted that he falls into the other category of those who are much harsher critics of themselves than others. He is much more likely to jump all over himself for making a mistake, and be less forgiving of the lapse, than he ever would be for a supervisee. Jon then asked the next question, about which case Michael would like to talk about.

SHE WAS DRIVING ME CRAZY

"What comes to mind is a picture of a woman that we'll call Mary. She is sitting across from me. She looks anxious. She is in her mid-30s, tall, thin, tense, a very nervous woman, very dependent. She had been referred to me by a colleague, a psychiatrist who had been giving her some medication. Supposedly, she just needed a session or two of support."

Hoyt explained that this case occurred 7 or 8 years ago but it still remained so vivid, so memorable, that it was as if he were still seeing her today. In fact, as he noted himself, sometimes even the verb tenses he uses become mixed when he is talking about her.

"Mary turned out to be very dependant and neurotic, something of a bottomless pit. She was a constant worrier and she had a diagnosis probably of generalized anxiety disorder (GAD) or depression not otherwise specified (NOS)—with anxious features. I don't think she had true obsessive–compulsive disorder (OCD) but she certainly had obsessive–compulsive personality features. But we will get to that.

"I was trying to be supportive and teach her some cognitive–behavior therapy (CBT) skills; ways to interrupt her worrying, challenge her premises and assumptions, learn relaxation techniques, that sort of stuff. This went on without any progress for several sessions."

Hoyt described trying to teach her some alternative ways to approach problems in her life, strategies that might reduce her anxiety and stress levels. He had tried relaxation training. He had tried challenging her irrational and distorted thinking. He had tried to get her to see that a lot of her misery was self-inflicted. He then continued:

"The moment I have in mind occurred after we had met several times. Whatever we were talking about she would deflect and ignore and then she would ask, '*But what if . . .*': 'What if there was an earthquake? What if my children get sick? What if my car won't work? What if my husband does leave me? What if my mother won't help? What if the pharmacy gives me the wrong medicine? What if . . . what if . . . what if.' She was driving me crazy.

"I answered patiently. I answered impatiently. I asked her to identify times she resisted the urge to worry. She ignored my questions, and the answers I had given her, and my efforts to redirect her. I asked her to reflect on why she kept asking the same questions in spite of having heard my answers. I asked her to consider what impact her repeated questionings had on me (and other people, like her husband and her kids). I shared with her my frustrations. I asked if she wanted to learn some other ways of thinking and responding."

The frustration in Michael's voice was still evident, even so many years later. It seemed that the harder he was working, and the more things he tried, the less effective he felt.

"Mary smiled at me and then resumed her litany of questions. Finally, after the umpteenth time I gently snapped. I stood up and announced that I would no longer be her therapist. I asked her to follow me to the front desk where she could sign up to see somebody else if she so desired. I remember her looking tearfully at me with a little glimmer of recognition in her eye that she had pushed me too far."

"You mean you won't see me anymore?" Mary asked Hoyt.

"That's right," he answered. "I'm not going to be able to see you anymore. Maybe someone else will, but not me."

Mary didn't make an appointment with another therapist. She said she wanted to think about it. After she left, Hoyt called the referring psychiatrist. "I felt like strangling him for referring her to me. He eventually called her and saw her himself."

UPON REFLECTION

Hoyt noted that confrontations like this can be therapeutic, even breakthroughs in otherwise stuck relationships. "But in this case I think my frustration and anger, while they may have dented her attention, didn't do so for long. I don't think I was helpful to her. I lost it and I lost the patient, too." Anticipating the next question, Hoyt answered before we could ask him what was hardest to him about this.

"What made the session so awful was the tension, my feeling of frustration and losing control, and that she went away feeling hurt and rejected. That certainly wasn't therapeutic at all." When asked what he learned from this case, Michael disclosed how difficult it was for him to talk about this.

"I'm not always helpful to clients, of course, but I don't often 'blow it' like that. Even now, while I'm imagining her sitting across from me, I begin to recall her voice and how nervous she was and I can still feel myself getting tense and wanting to escape. It's embarrassing to talk about how untherapeutic I was, how unkind I was."

Hoyt was concerned that by being so honest and forthcoming about his "bad therapy" session people might think that this was typical of him. We reminded him that we had seen him work effectively and consistently before, sometimes doing clinical demonstrations in very public settings (such as conferences and on videotapes). We easily agreed with him that it was very hard to talk about the worst parts of our work. We also reassured him, and ourselves, that we believe colleagues will welcome with open arms those of us who are courageous enough to risk talking about this forbidden subject.

"So," Hoyt continued, "What did I learn? I learned that I didn't have a clear therapeutic alliance and contract with her—it didn't feel like we were working together. Clearly, my getting so aggravated and taking it personally, rather than seeing this process as part of her problem, that was a mistake. I remember one of my supervisors once saying that 'Therapy would be easy if the patients weren't neurotic!' I was sort of expecting that she would always be cooperative and everything would go easily."

Jon then remarked, "Of course, it would go easier still if *we* weren't neurotic as well."

"Yeah—we're about to get to that," Michael replied. "I realize that if I wasn't going to continue seeing her I certainly could have found a more graceful way of ending therapy and extricating myself rather than standing up and firing her, humiliating her, and making her feel bad. I set her up to make it even harder for her to see another therapist.

"I've learned a couple of things from this. One is that if someone is pushing my buttons, or therapy isn't being useful, I need to regroup. I should consult with a colleague. I should try something different. I find that if someone is making me crazy, or I feel allergic to him or her, I'm very unlikely to do much good. I think a clue is when I look at my schedule and see a certain name and go 'Oh, crap!' or get that sinking, dreadful feeling, I think it is time to do something quickly. If I'm feeling this way, then the client is probably feeling it, too. They know they are not going to be well received and we are not getting anywhere good.

"Another thing I learned is that I shouldn't have accepted Mary as my client without being prepared. It's important to know your triggers. I can certainly see things in my own personal history and personality that made me more vulnerable to doing poorly with a highly anxious and dependant female patient. I don't think that means that I or other people shouldn't work with such folks—you might even have a certain passion or empathy for them—but it does mean we have to find ways to make sure that our own issues don't get activated in an antitherapeutic way. I think it's important that if you see a pattern in your impasses or failures, to look at your own role. This term *resistance* is too easily applied to patients. I think we should first look at our contribution as therapists, and then look at the interpersonal process, and then, only then, look at the client. Everybody may be playing a role but I think that blaming the client is an easy way out, kind of like hating the ball or throwing your clubs in golf."

SPECIAL VISION

Characteristic of many brief therapists who see their role as making therapy work, Hoyt accepts full responsibility in negative outcomes. Apart from this one case he presented, we wondered about his most typical or recurrent weaknesses as a clinician throughout his career.

"I think there is a fine line between where I try to empathize and see things through other people's eyes, versus becoming totally absorbed in their worlds. I see their logic and join with them, sometimes to the point that I get stuck. Just like them, I won't see options. I get stuck the same way they get stuck. So I need to keep a certain objectivity, a delicate balance between being a part of and apart from. I can be sensitive and empathic but I think it's important to have a different perspective from theirs."

"You become overly empathic?"

"Well, the idea is that it's supposed to be stereoscopic vision. You get a depth perception with two different perspectives. If you only have one perspective—the client's—then you may not be able to help them to see things that they don't already see.

"I was thinking about this in terms of other cases. I treat lots of people who have OCD and anxiety disorders and they don't all make me crazy, so it's not just highly anxious people or nervous women or something like that."

Hoyt explained that this particular case with Mary became personal for him to a point where he lost his special vision, his "degrees of freedom," that would allow him to help her break out of the same dysfunctional pattern. "Sometimes when I have been too close to a problem because it's part of my life, it becomes harder to be therapeutic. When I was a much younger therapist, the issues I was dealing with in my own life made it harder for me to have a long view on young people coming in with those sorts of problems. I'm noticing, now that I'm in my mid-50s, that I'm seeing lots of people who are having midlife issues and talking about retirement and finding meaning and all these sort of things. It certainly resonates with some of the things going on in my own life. I have to be careful that I am not projecting my stuff onto clients and interacting with them in a way that forces them to identify with it and take it on."

Hoyt sees these blind spots as the main area that he most has to watch out for to protect himself and his clients from mistakes he has made in the past. Although brief therapy may be his specialty, he noted that he has been thinking and writing about these countertransference issues, from a variety of perspectives, for a long time.

"I look back and I think about people I saw a long time ago and I realize that I didn't know squat. What was I doing with those people? I'm sure that there are other people I see now and I'm unaware of things I do that I won't like years from now."

Hoyt mentions that there is a flip side to this as well. "One time I did a lot of work with grief and another time I was very interested in eating disorders. I had a passion for it and it was very exciting and I was doing a lot of work with those folks. Now I still have some interest but I have moved on. I've been there and done that and I'm not as turned on by those kind of problems. So I think sometimes we may have blind spots but sometimes we may have special vision where we are really lit up or excited about something and we can go farther with it."

EVEN GOOD THERAPISTS MAKE MISTAKES

Asking Michael to expand beyond his own experiences, we wondered what he thought other therapists should be doing to deal with their mistakes and failures more constructively.

"I am supervising a small group of therapists and there is a mixture in some situations where you may have both a clinical supervisory and an administrative role. I've said to my little group that I am only willing to do clinical supervision under the agreement that I can indicate to the department administrator that we have been meeting but in no way will I say anything evaluative about who is good, or who is bad, or who we should hire, and so on. The one exception, of course, is if someone is doing something so clumsy or unethical that it's endangering patients. I think it would be very hard for people to talk about problems or mistakes or anything like that if they feel that it's going to cost them a job or a promotion or something like that. It's hard enough to talk about this stuff candidly.

"The therapists like that and I honor that with them. Many years ago I gave a presentation at a large medical center about a transference–countertransference problem I was having with a patient. I showed some videotape of a particularly sticky moment. It was a large audience; maybe a couple of hundred people. Afterward about 20 people came up to talk to me. I'm sure a few wanted to give me their card and offer me a therapy appointment [*laughs*] but most of them wanted to come up and thank me for opening the space for discussions about when things don't go well. I was thinking about this because I knew we were going to do this interview. It encouraged me when I remembered that someone had even said to me, 'If you, an obviously intelligent and highly competent therapist, if you can get stuck and make mistakes it makes me feel that it's okay for me to admit this, too.' Otherwise it is sort of a shameful thing; it's a dirty little secret."

Hoyt mentioned that in one of his recent books, *Some Stories Are Better than Others*, he included a chapter about the therapeutic failures of the famous psychiatrist and hypnotherapist, Milton Erickson. "I collected all the published reports and reviewed the cases. Dr. Erickson was a genius, and I like to read about successes and I have learned concepts and techniques that I can model and adapt in my own work, but sometimes reading and seeing brilliant success and miracle cure after miracle cure leaves me feeling disempowered. I walk away thinking 'I could never do that.' So I think it's good to know that there really is a range. I think that is an important thing: to know that even good therapists make mistakes.

"Having a bad episode or a bad therapy doesn't mean that you are a bad therapist or that you are a bad person. One shouldn't overgeneralize. Some snapshots from a trip really only depict a split second and not the entire journey. I think if you are having lots of bad therapy sessions then you had better take a look at what is going on because there is some problem there. But I think if you are having bad ones on rare occasions, hey, that's what we all do."

Chapter 21

RICHARD B. STUART
I Expect Too Much

RICHARD B. STUART was among the first researchers to investigate failures in therapy. In his book, *Trick or Treatment*, he explored the circumstances under which negative outcomes take place. That alone would have been a significant contribution to our field, but Stuart has distinguished himself in a number of other areas, each of which has evolved from his previous work.

Stuart was originally trained in the Sullivanian psychoanalytic tradition. But during his training, he had a growing awareness of two major problems. The first was the profound focus on psychopathology that led analysts to ignore many aspects of adaptive functioning. And the second was the difficulty in operationally defining key analytic terms, which made objective assessment of its outcome all but impossible. After moving to the University of Michigan from New York, where he completed his doctoral work, he studied and became strongly identified with the emerging behavior-therapy movement. He first applied social learning theory in his work with juvenile delinquents, their families, and their schools, in an effort to maintain in the community those who would otherwise have been institutionalized. Growing out of this work was his development of protocols for work with couples and families. This work led to his writing the classic treatise on behavioral marital therapy that became a well-worn resource for clinicians interested in utilizing specific homework assignments as part of their helping efforts. In *Helping Couples Change*, several of the methods introduced became part of almost every therapist's repertoire.

Stuart next turned his efforts toward applying behavioral methods, as well as other strategies he developed, for treating obesity. In *Slim Chance in a Fat World*, *Act Thin, Stay Thin*, and *Weight, Sex, and Marriage*, he provided both professionals and the public with an integrated approach for addressing excessive eating, as well as the underlying meaning of this behavior.

Finally, Stuart has turned his attention to several other important clinical areas in books he has authored or coauthored: *Adherence, Compliance, and Generalization in Behavioral Medicine, Second Marriage,* and *Violent Behavior: Social Learning Approaches to Prediction, Management, and Treatment.* This last book is directly related to his current practice in which he sees a number of high-risk couples who have been embroiled in patterns of physical or emotional abuse.

Stuart is Emeritus Professor of Psychiatry at the University of Washington, Seattle and also teaches and directs the program offering respecialization in Clinical Psychology at the Fielding Graduate Institute.

A CONTINUUM OF BAD THERAPY

Dick Stuart had spent considerable time organizing his thoughts and writing down some ideas prior to our conversation. Although we were grateful for his reflective and thoughtful efforts, Stuart apologized if he came across in a lecturing style. Jon knew from prior collaborations with Stuart that this style helped him to remain clear and focused so we let him direct his own interview by following the agenda he had prepared. Stuart began by addressing the first question we had asked: What bad therapy means to him.

"I have to differentiate unsuccessful therapy from bad therapy. I think it is important to think about both of those as dimensional and not categorical. There is a continuum from less than optimal at one end to quite harmful at the other. Unsuccessful therapy fails to meet all goals or the stated goal at the hoped-for level of change. Some positive changes may result, but not at the level that might have been accomplished through better planned and executed therapy. Its ill effects are delaying the onset of change, wasting the clients' time and money, and possibly discouraging the client from seeking subsequent therapy. In contrast, the bad therapy can make matters worse by triggering latent pathology as a result of overtaxing clients' coping skills, it can inadvertently instigate maladaptive behavior, and it can harmfully disrupt family and community contacts that would otherwise have been resources for the client."

Stuart referred back to the case of treatment failure he presented in *Trick or Treatment* earlier in his career. "That kid was an interesting example of both of my definitions. What he experienced at his school was a combination of both unsuccessful and bad therapy. The school kept him out of a normal educational route for 3 years for no justifiable reason, which resulted in unnecessary developmental delays. It was harmful because it convinced the child and his family that there were pathological problems that could not be overcome both in the boy and his interaction with his parents and grandmother. When I wrote about that case I really had a kind of messianic zeal about it because I viewed this undermining focus on pathology and failure to establish and monitor behavior-change goals as being highly destructive."

WHO GETS TO DECIDE WHAT IS GOOD OR BAD?

This point about meeting expectations gets us thinking about how the ultimate evaluation is determined: Who decides whether the therapy has been successful or not? "Often clients and therapists have very different criteria," Stuart said. "It amazes me that sometimes I get referrals of friends and relatives from clients whose therapy I thought was quite unsuccessful, yet these supposed failures told laudatory stories to others about my work."

We laughed appreciatively because this very point had been at the forefront of our own efforts to define failure. There are times when our consumers could not be happier with the result, even though we can't see a single change in their behavior or reduction of their symptoms. Other confusing situations present us with clients who complain incessantly about how unsatisfied they are with our work yet it is obvious for all to see how much they have profited.

Illustrating this very point, Dick talked about some of his experience in helping people lose weight. "One of the problems is that obese patients don't necessarily begin therapy because they want to change. Instead, many of them would like to do exactly what they are already doing but have different outcomes. The model of obesity treatment that I developed and worked with for many years was a two-component model. One assumption is that obesity serves a function, and overeating serves a function, and they are different. Both problems must be solved through a meaningful process of self-change if an overweight person is to substantially lose weight."

Stuart went on to explain some of the functions of obesity as a form of social engineering. He mentioned that such patients may immunize themselves from unwanted sexual advances or use their excessive weight as an excuse for not taking care of other things in their lives. He also points out that overeating is the most universally abused mood-controlling substance.

"Most of the obese people that I work with primarily experience one emotion, which is hunger. If they were depressed it was immediately translated into hunger. If they were happy, it was immediately translated into hunger. If they were anxious—hunger. Bored? Hunger. So what you have to do is help people differentiate between their emotions. Rather than trying to help them find a better remedy for these feelings, my proactive approach calls for motivating clients to change the situations that trigger these problem emotions.

"I would see a lot of women who would come in for four or five sessions. Basically they wanted to tell their story. They wanted to be heard. They hoped to find foods that were less troublesome than the ones that contributed to their obesity, but they were rarely ready to take the risks that were necessary to overcome their problems. If they felt understood, they often left happy: someone listened to their story and they felt validated. But they acquired no skills that would empower them to meet the many challenges of successful weight management."

We smiled at this paradox, imagining these clients who wanted a Carl Rogers and got a Dick Stuart instead. It was a testimony to Stuart's flexibility that he was willing to do this kind of relationship-oriented, affirming work when it went against his notions of what his clients really needed. Even though his clients left completely satisfied with the outcome—even though they didn't lost any weight—Stuart considered these treatment ventures to have been quite unsuccessful.

"There is a subtext in therapy that makes it hard to decide when it succeeds and when it does not because the stated goals are not necessarily the actual goals. For this subset of overweight women, it was sufficient for them to be able to say that they had gone to this expert in the hope that significant others in their lives would therefore be more forebearing. Nevertheless, I considered the therapy to have been a sorry failure."

CRITERIA FOR EVALUATING OUTCOMES

Given this confusing state of affairs, we asked Stuart how he reconciled these different assessments of what constitutes good and bad therapy. How did he deal with the discrepancies between his own and his clients' expectations for success?

"I try to evaluate the therapy using several criteria. First of all: Did I connect? Did I create an interaction in which clients could tell their story and I could feel some reasonable certainty about being able to see the world through their eyes? In other words, could I enter their system? Were they relaxed enough, and forthcoming enough, to let me in?"

Gee, Stuart *had* changed a lot since his early days as such a passionate advocate of behaviorism. This was not surprising, of course, since his work in couples therapy has always involved an integrative approach that valued the quality of relationships.

Stuart emphasized that therapy sometimes didn't work because he was unable to establish a strong alliance with the clients. He found it difficult to accept them, or relate to them, or to understand their worldview.

There were other situations in which the client may have considered the therapy to be useless but Dick believed that the treatment was a success. This is especially the case with some of the high-risk couples he sees who present problems related to violence or abuse issues.

"It is not unusual for a woman to say that she realizes that her husband is abusive but she feels that it is her obligation to learn to deal with the situation. Sometimes partners of abusive men state that they are seeking therapy to learn how to accept and forgive their husband's violence. That's a contract to which I cannot agree because the behavior is, in my judgment, inherently destructive and antisocial. The best that I could do is to tell them that while I understood what they wanted to accomplish, I considered it to be a goal that works to no one's advantage. It would not help the abuser if he were enabled to continue to act in this dysfunctional way, it has a severely pathogenic impact on the wife, and it's terrible modeling for the children."

Stuart judged the therapy successful if the wife was simply open to talking about these issues and willing to consider another way of viewing the abuse and violence. "A fair number of the women would leave and say they were sorry I couldn't help them. They would consider the therapy a failure but I would consider it successful because perhaps for the first time a question was raised in a way that could empower them to come to a different answer sometime in the future."

Stuart saw two important issues that emerged from this experience that were important for therapists to consider. One was the need for each therapist to be aware of his or her moral limits with respect to clients' goals and the steps needed to reach them. He believed that therapists are not entitled to impose their values on their clients, but at the same time, therapists must not pervert their own values for the sake of clients' desires to seek unwholesome goals. The second is the need for therapists to know the limits of their competency and to refrain from attempting to provide every service sought by clients. He believed that practice beyond their skill level is one of the most common causes of bad therapy, as when therapists who are trained only in individual therapy attempt to use the same techniques with couples and families who require very different methods.

PREDICTIONS AND POSTCARDS

Directing the conversation from the general to specific cases, we asked Stuart what it was like to spend time thinking about bad therapy and reflecting on his failures in anticipation for this interview. Just as we do in therapy, we have found that some of the best stuff emerges between the lines—the parts that were not predicted or anticipated. Given Stuart's logical and systematic nature, we wondered what the reflective process was like for him during the preceding weeks.

Dick admitted that the exercise was interesting but not that different from what he does all the time anyway.

"I keep a fair amount of follow-up data on clients who have allowed me into their lives. For many years I sent people an annual postcard following up interventions that had been terminated. I played a game with myself when I did this, wanting to estimate the accuracy of my predictions about the effectiveness of the intervention at the last session as found in the endnote for each treatment effort. It's interesting to get these postcards back 1, 2, 3, as many as 5 years later. I am able to reconcile this feedback with my own judgment."

In examining the data that he has collected over the years, Stuart has found that the failures could be divided into several categories. First were those cases in which he tried to be too parental and directive. In such cases, he was not successful in helping clients establish their own goals. He became too prescriptive and overstructured. Next were those cases in which the client entered therapy as a result of trying to please or appease another person; motivation for change was minimal. The presented agenda may have been deceptive since the client really had little interest in changing anything, other than to get someone else off his or her back.

A third category of clients he struggled with were those who were a bit out of control. "Some people were so paralyzed that they were only willing to use emotion-focused coping strategies. They were completely unwilling to use problem-focused methods. The emotion-focused ones primarily want to talk about how bad they feel. I think that can be a useful sidebar in therapy but should in no way be a primary function of the treatment. It always frustrates me when I can't help clients move beyond thinking about how bad they feel into discussing what they can do to change their feelings."

This is one reason why Stuart stopped working with alcoholics, whom he found to be too infatuated with viewing themselves as victims. "They wanted a great deal of commiseration, but they don't want to see themselves as the cocreator of the experiences that they believed led them to 'need a drink.' The model that I use is much more proactive than that. I would feel an incredible strain and disappointment after sessions with alcoholics and realized that my style was rarely likely to be of help to them."

This was a particularly good example of what Stuart meant when he said it was critical for clinicians to know their limits, their weaknesses, and to try not to be and do all things for all people. This philosophy was consistent with the ways he helped couples as well.

"I don't think that every couple that comes into my office brings a marriage made in heaven. I think that some couples are together for the wrong reasons and would be much better served by being either independent or with other people. I try to help partners to agree on criteria for their relationship, take steps to achieve these criteria, and then evaluate whether or not to stay in that relationship only if it is satisfying enough to warrant that decision."

HOW AND WHY I FAIL

Talking further about when and how he had failed with couples, Stuart mentioned several rather clear principles.

"I fail if couples leave without being willing to try and work things out. I also fail if they stay in the relationship even though they are still very unhappy. I succeed if they make an attempt to change and decide that while better, their relationship is still not good enough to be preserved. And I succeed if the partners stay together because they have found a new level of satisfaction."

We noticed that Stuart clearly accepted responsibility for the outcomes in his work. The pronoun *I* indicated that it was his job to structure things in such a way that the clients left satisfied, but also that he felt satisfied with the result. This was in marked contrast to other practitioners who favored the pronoun, we" or even those who see the outcome as determined primarily by the client's commitment and motivation. It was not that Dick did not take these factors into consideration, but he was not willing to let himself off the hook and blame the client if things didn't work out.

"Some of my marital failures are more likely to be with people who go through a change process and don't come to a logical conclusion. These are people who don't say, 'We are crying ourselves to sleep every night. This isn't where we really ought to be. But we are exhausted and don't have hope of a better life elsewhere, so we'll unhappily stay where we are.'" Stuart becomes very frustrated with these cases and very disappointed in the way things work out. He feels sad that some people settled for such mediocrity in their love relationships.

THE SHOELACE PRINCIPLE

Stuart was quite realistic about what can and cannot be accomplished in therapy, especially in his work with couples, and particularly with those who manifest abuse or violence. But there is a problem in all work with couples inherent in the fact that the partners are individuals who are invested in preserving and justifying their personal styles. As a result, few partners begin therapy in a mood to compromise; rather, most come in hoping that the therapist will ally with them in efforts to change their mates. As a result, it is altogether rare that both partners are satisfied with any session, no matter how much progress was made. This is what he calls "the shoelace principle."

"You change one person in order to facilitate a change in the other person, and it goes back and forth. In each one of those sessions the person who changes often feels put upon. I see it as quite the reverse. Anybody who I can help make a change I have helped get closer to achieving what he or she wants. I expect people to be really appreciative and yet they rarely are. They only become appreciative when the other partner begins to change. That makes assessing couples interventions difficult on a week-by-week basis. It also reinforces one of my notions that when I fail in couples therapy, it's because I have overidentified with the victim and probably colluded to change the putative bad guy."

In his role as savior, Stuart has tried to equalize the power in the relationship by siding with the victim. In such circumstances he has failed to develop a strong enough alliance with the more powerful partner who then may not stay in therapy. It takes two shoelaces to tie a shoe and keep it tight.

COUNTERTRANSFERENCE AND LEAVING HOME

"What about a specific case when this situation occurred," we asked Stuart. "What is a time when you overidentified with the victim and lost the other partner as an active participant in the process?"

"I am currently seeing a woman who is a highly successful professional. She has an extremely high-level job. She bites her husband very severely when she gets angry. These are not love bites. She draws blood. She has also stabbed her husband with a paring knife on several occasions."

"So, what is that like for you?"

"I kept putting myself in the guy's position and it seemed to me it was a terribly sad position to be in. The guy has some mild handicaps that I don't think are impairing in the least but he thinks they were undermining his potential for success in life. That led him to feel that he had few options and was therefore quite dependent on this woman for financial and social reasons."

Stuart realized that he had no sympathy whatsoever for the wife. He was unable to empathize with her, nor feel much in the way of support of her position. Once he realized the extent of his strong negative feelings he also accepted that he was probably going to lose the couple.

"One of the inner dialogues that plays out in my mind is the constant questioning of whether I have a balanced connection with both partners. Have I fallen into the trap of seeing one as Satan incarnate and the other as an angel? Anytime I do that, the therapy is going to fail unless I can do a midcourse correction. It's not going to work because I am going to either fail to suggest the remedies that I would with other couples, or I will impose a perspective on them."

Stuart went on to point out that he realized that every one of his clients feels justified in thinking, feeling, and acting as they do. He believes that his ability to be helpful is limited by the extent to which he can "enter the client's system," framing options for change in terms meaningful to his clients. When he distances himself from would-be Satanic clients, he precludes his opportunity to experience this quintessential empathy.

A similar pattern plays itself out when Stuart works with families in which he overidentifies with the children.

"How is it that this happens?" we ask him.

"I left home when I was 14," Dick says. "I don't see parents as necessarily assets in their children's lives."

Stuart mentioned his personal history so casually that we almost overlooked the opening and allowed the conversation to continue on purely an intellectual level. We asked him if he wouldn't mind saying more about what caused him to leave home when he was so young.

"I just had strange parents. I was dyslexic and I did terribly in school. And my parents were nutcases. The last day of school one year one of my friends and I decided we would see where we could go. So we started to hitchhike. I ended up hitchhiking to Idaho as a wrangler and living on the fringe of the world in which I grew up for the next several years."

Stuart began to resume the previous narrative and left us hanging with his story. We pressed him to finish what happened next, how he managed to raise himself from the age of 14, surviving by his wits. We wondered about the connections between his personal history and his devotion to helping conflicted couples work out their difficulties. There were some familiar threads in our own childhood backgrounds.

Dick admitted that his childhood experiences in such a dysfunctional home had made him particularly unsympathetic to people who wallow in their misery. "For some people, wallowing is the best they can do. I know that I may be too quick to act and I also may expect too much from them."

PRINCESS AND THE PEA EFFECT

We challenged Stuart about the possibility of being able to help to meet his own high expectations. "Of course I'm supposed to be able to help everybody! I get paid to help them. The expectation has got to be that I can help everybody even though the reality is that I can't."

Stuart made the point again that his main problem when working with families was his tendency to villainize parents. He leaned toward thinking that many parents are overcontrolling with their kids.

"I had done this study in Ann Arbor in the mid-1960s that reached a conclusion that I termed "The Princess and the Pea Effect." Most parents are so significantly underreinforcing with their children and so selective in what they do reinforce. They reinforce what pleases them, not what works well for the kid. I really find it easy to fall in the trap of being the child's savior and not the family's therapist."

Because his own life experiences had led him to believe that family environments were not safe places, and that parents were not often competent, he must watch carefully his inclination to serve as a rescuer. "I think that there is a profound risk of narcissism in us all to assume that our internal working models are somehow the measures of truth in life. Along with all therapists, I have a never-ending struggle to avoid imposing on my clients the perceptions and beliefs that have guided decisions that I have made through the years."

RAINBOWS AND STORMS

When we asked Stuart to select one case of bad therapy to talk about in detail, he admitted that he found it difficult to settle on just one. "But I can identify a class of bad experiences to make it generic." He thought of a couple named Alice and Ben. He had been far more successful in connecting with the wife than he had with the husband. Like most of his first sessions, which he calls the "honeymoon," things went pretty well. It was the in the second session that real trouble started.

"Alice had stayed on the phone for 30 minutes after Ben had come home from work. She had been talking to one of her girlfriends whose mother had died. Ben got mad, swore at her, slammed the door, and went out for a few hours. When he got home he had had too much to drink but he was very contrite. That happened the night before our session. "The next day they came in and when I asked what was going on there was silence for awhile. Then Alice said they'd had an argument last night. She got about four sentences into it when Ben interrupted her."

"'You always have to have things your way,' Ben insisted. 'You never see my point of view. It's hopeless and I just want out.'"

"When you say 'out' what do you mean?" Stuart asked him trying to shift the direction of the conversation. Ben continued to berate and verbally abuse Alice in the session, with Stuart trying to act as a referee. Alice kept stressing that she would like to work things out but the harder she tried, the more Ben stubbornly refused.

"Ben," Stuart pressed him, "let's talk about what you mean by 'getting out.' Does that mean you want to move out now? Does that mean you want a divorce? Do you want a separation? What exactly does *out* mean?"

"I just don't want anything to do with her."

"Okay," Stuart calmed him. "Alice, if Ben moves out, how will you cope? You have two kids. What are you going to do?" They talked about these options for about 2 minutes before Ben got up, announced he didn't want to listen to this any more, and then he walked out the door.

"Over the next 3 or 4 days," Stuart explains, "Ben phoned my office at least a dozen times to say Alice was throwing him out. He said he really loved her and now wanted to be with her. He asked me to act as his advocate and try to get Alice to relent. It was painful, but I told him that I couldn't speak for him, and I was afraid that Alice had already heard and clearly understood the message that he had sent."

Stuart asked himself what went wrong. "Usually when I fail, I fail in the second session. There is a more benign class of failures that happens later. Sometimes couples are not satisfied with the rate of progress. Or they can be too satisfied and leave after accomplishing some changes but before they have had a chance to consolidate and fully integrate the skills needed to maintain the changes."

What bothered Dick most about this case was that he felt blindsided. "I do strength-oriented assessments so I am at a risk of overlooking Axis II problems. When patients initially overreact, I tend to look at it as a lack of emotional intelligence. If it persists, I label it an *attachment disorder*. I am loath to go to the next step and think about it as a characterological problem, and that is because they are so difficult to resolve. They overwhelm any chance of progress that I am going to make until they are addressed. So many partners are seduced by the rainbows that follow the storms.

"With this guy, I missed the Axis II features. What I really should have done in the first session was to be sensitive to that and say that while I was glad that they wanted to make progress as a couple, there were some things I think they had to work on individually first. It would have been a mistake to say to Ben that he was the problem, so I would have had to say to both of them that there were goals that should be accomplished by each one individually as a precursor to being able to change as a couple. And I would say it's best to talk about those separately and not together. That is because you have to be very careful not to provide them with language that can be used coercively in arguments that follow. So the mistake that I still make sometimes is missing severe Axis II pathology. I am too much of a Pollyanna."

We agreed that one that thing that most contributed to Stuart's success—his optimism and hope—also led him to fail at times because he gave people the benefit of the doubt.

REVISITING THE EXPERIENCES

Thinking back over these episodes Stuart still felt a degree of discomfort. "Since I am in the business to help people and improve the quality of their lives, I really feel a mixture of embarrassment and sorrow. I'm embarrassed that my thinking was so flawed. I'm sorry because I do sometimes overidentify and because after 40 years of doing therapy, I should be even better at catching Axis II pathologies than I am. I still get taken in because the personality disorders can be ingratiating."

We asked Dick to consider what he learned from the case. "When I go back over this Ben and Alice thing—which was a relatively recent case by the way—I have to remind myself to curb my enthusiasm for my own protocol. I have such confidence in what I can do that it sometimes overwhelms the facts. As I look back on the first session, I didn't feel that I connected with Ben. That should have been a signal to me and I ignored it. I figured that I could help anybody. I believed that I could help 100% of the couples I see have a better relationship. And I love doing that. But I didn't ask myself if this relationship could offer everyone in the family all that they deserve. They came in saying they wanted to stay together and I took that at face value without asking myself the questions that could have led me to choose a wiser approach."

"Some therapists would say that you are not supposed to be God and accept those kinds of decisions," Jon challenged Stuart.

"But remember that I am paid as an expert. They come to me because they assume I know more about their situation then they do. I accept that belief. If I take that path, I have a responsibility to deliver on the promise."

WHAT I REGRET

Looking back over his career, we asked Stuart about his regrets, or what he could have done differently. "One of my biggest mistakes in the first 20 years of my career was to subscribe to 'isms.' I started out as a Sullivanian analyst for 10 years, then I was a radical behaviorist; both are narrow positions. I wished that I had started thinking more pragmatically and integratively. I would have done better therapy over the years." He went on to explain that he believed that he downplayed the importance of personality factors such as internal models and attachment orientation because of his own life experience. He wanted to believe that he changed who he was by changing the world in which he lived, and that clients could readily do the same. "I do believe that people can change much more radically than they ever thought possible, but I now realize that change is easiest to accomplish if the efforts to achieve it blend an understanding of personal vulnerabilities, personal skills, and environmental situations that bring out the worst and best in people. My goal then becomes helping them challenge internal reactions that cause problems, develop a repertoire that allows them to create the relationships that work best for them, and then empower them to create and maintain these relationships."

Chapter 22

MICHELE WEINER-DAVIS
Struck by a Bolt
of Lightning—Again!

MICHELE WEINER-DAVIS is one of the contributors to the development of solution-focused therapy, a model she later adapted to work
with troubled couples. After a first book for therapists (*In Search
of Solutions*), she has since helped launch the popularity of brief
therapy with a succession of books addressed to the public: *Change
Your Life and Everyone In It, Getting Through to the Man You
Love, The Divorce Remedy,* and the influential *Divorce Busting.*

Weiner-Davis works out of her Divorce Busting Center in the
Chicago area where she maintains an active private practice and
consulting business.

I DON'T HANG ONTO THINGS

As one of the first advocates of brief therapy aimed at solving specific,
symptomatic problems, we knew that with Weiner-Davis's work it would
be relatively easy to determine whether the treatment would be good or
bad: either the solution offered worked well or it did not. Period. We
thus imagined that she would have a whole long list of mostly successes,
but also quite a few failures inscribed in her memory. We were wrong.

Michele was quite intrigued with the project and very much wanted
to participate. The difficulty she saw, however, was that it was hard for
her to settle on a particular example of bad therapy. In fact, it was hard
for her to remember details of failure at all, and this intrigued her.

"I was thinking back over all these years I have been working with
people and I know I have had lots and lots of failures like everyone else.
I even show some of my mistakes at my workshops. But the truth is that

when I started to think about whether I could give you any detail on any of those cases, the answer is no.

"I started wondering what was wrong with me. Am I not being introspective enough? Am I not giving careful enough thought to things that I could improve? I started being concerned about this."

It was perhaps not surprising that one of the earliest advocates of "reframing problems" and "looking for exceptions" would approach this dilemma by seeing things from a new light. "I flipped things around and I asked myself if you had invited me to do a similar thing on my great successes—some people's names, and the positive feelings I'd had about them, do come to mind. But again, I couldn't tell you about the details of the case, nor why I thought the case was successful. I don't hang onto things. I particularly don't hang onto things that I think are failures."

Wow. With so much denial related to our subject, it was refreshing to hear such honesty. But before we could remark on this, Michele continued, explaining what she does do after each and every session—a quick mental review of the case. It may take a few minutes, or even span the course of the following week. "I take some cases home with me," she said.

During this period of reflection, she reviewed what went wrong and planned to make adjustments immediately, both in the specific ways she might work with the clients next time, and also in her overall style.

"The next time they come back, I do something different. I guess I believe that the only real failure in therapy is when you don't keep your eyes and heart open so that you continue to make the same kind of mistake over and over again. I truly learn from each session."

THERE'S LOTS OF BAD THERAPY

Of course, Weiner-Davis was describing exactly what she teaches others to do in therapy. One of the main thrusts of her work is quite simply to help people to figure out what they are doing that is not working and then to get them to try something different. No wonder she doesn't hang onto her mistakes, nor give much lingering thought to failure: these concepts are not consistent with the way she thinks.

However, eventually she was able to recall a case that would illustrate what we were after—examples of bad therapy. "Actually, two cases that came to mind that I want to talk about—one was really funny and the other, not quite so funny."

Before she launched into the stories, Michele wanted us to know the context for her remarks and what feelings and thoughts she had about doing this. For someone who is known primarily for being so pragmatic and action-oriented, it seemed surprising that she is so reflective and warm in the conversations.

A BOLT OF LIGHTNING

"The case that I said was kind of humorous happened many years ago. I was working at a social service agency. I was one of the head honchos there and we used to work with a team approach with a one-way mirror."

Weiner-Davis doesn't recall if a team was watching this particular family but she does remember some of the details about the family. The father was very domineering in the sessions, quite a handful for the neophyte that Michele was at the time. They had come for help because of difficulty with their teenaged daughter.

"I really felt that the father was not recognizing his daughter's strengths. He was very critical. I made some headway with the family and things were getting better, but then they hit a plateau. After several sessions of no improvement, they dropped out."

However, a year later the family returned to the agency. Only this time they were going to work with one of Weiner-Davis' colleagues and she would sit behind the one-way mirror, watch the proceedings, and get a different perspective on the case. This seemed to her to be the best of all possible worlds.

"My colleague joined very well with the father and things seemed to be going along okay. But again, a similar thing happened. After a few productive sessions, they got stuck again. I was sitting behind the mirror watching this unfold when I was struck by a bolt of lightning. This incredibly creative idea came over me and I could not believe that I had missed it before. It was a wonderful reframe."

The therapist working with the family took his usual break so he could consult with Weiner-Davis and a few others sitting behind the mirror. Michele could barely restrain herself, she was so excited about her insight.

"I don't know how I missed this last time I worked with them but I really feel I have it. I have this incredible reframe that weaves together all the pieces of this family dynamic in a wonderful tapestry. I want you to write this down word for word." Weiner-Davis then waited impatiently while the therapist took out a pen and paper to comply with her request. Meanwhile, she was concentrating as hard as she could to make sure she didn't lose a single precious word of this complex solution. She dictated the procedure exactly. Rarely had she ever felt so confident.

"The therapist wrote down the message to the family like a good soldier. I spelled everything out for him—it was rather long. Then he went back into the room. We all just sat there breathlessly, waiting in anticipation of how the intervention would be received by the family."

The therapist went through the points one by one, performing beautifully and making sure to hit each crucial point. Weiner-Davis thought that things were going pretty well. She noted that the family, and remarkably, even the father, were all listening politely, making eye contact, nodding their heads. The father didn't even interrupt, which was a very good sign indeed. Finally, the therapist was done reading the intervention, word for word. The father looked at him, cocked his head, and said: "Look, we were here a year ago and that woman, Michele Weiner-Davis, told us the same thing. We didn't buy it *then* and we don't buy it *now*."

"Oh God," Michele muttered aloud, feeling terrible for her colleague who was stuck in the room to sort this all out. We laughed appreciatively. This *was* a funny story, but also one that reminded us of our own similar lapses. The main difference was that we don't often work in front of a one-way mirror with our colleagues watching.

I FINALLY LISTENED

Back to the story, Weiner-Davis elaborated: "I obviously didn't keep very good notes because I probably should have remembered that." This case reminded her of when she was a much younger, less experienced therapist. "I was so wrapped up in technique and taken with it. I fell in love with the strategies I was trained to use. I wasn't always listening to the family. I wasn't always listening to what I was telling them."

Michele told us that she thought it was very important for beginning therapists to have a fairly structured conceptual framework for working with people, but not to the point where this model became more important than the clients you were trying to help. "If you are so enamored with your techniques, you forget to listen to and watch your clients. That's a problem."

This, then, reminded her of the second case she wanted to discuss, one that she found more illuminating. Since the session was videotaped, she often shows it at workshops to demonstrate how to work with resistant couples. "I used to show this tape to illustrate a particular technique that I favored. It only dawned on me recently that what actually accounts for the positive shift in this case wasn't use of the technique at all. Things changed when I finally listened to the guy! Now I show this tape as an example of what happens in therapy when you rely too heavily on technique and stop listening to your clients."

PLAYING WITH FEELING

We were excited to hear about Michele's evolution from being technique oriented to a position of valuing more the core conditions of a helping relationship from which those interventions take place. Again, in these interviews we learned so much more about these master therapists than what is published in their books. This second case illustrates quite a different facet of Michele from what we ordinarily associate with her work.

"Let me start the story at the end point and then work my way backwards. As a kid, I took piano lessons. I remember that when I would go for my lessons my piano teacher would sometimes say, 'Michele, you have to play this with feeling. Play softer and louder and use the pedals. Put your heart into it.'" When Weiner-Davis paused for dramatic effect, we both smiled as we heard the beginning of what we knew would be a great metaphor.

"I remember thinking to myself that I can't play the piece with feeling until I get the notes down. In other words, because I hadn't practiced, I was really concentrating hard on reading the music and putting my fingers where they were supposed to be. If I had practiced more ahead of time, I could really have gotten into it."

This is exactly what she had found to be true when practicing therapy. Once you have the notes down, once you know the finger positions, once you can read the music effortlessly, then, and only then, can you play with feeling. "This becomes what more seasoned therapists often talk about as the 'art' of doing therapy."

It was for this reason that Michele no longer liked to do workshops in which she teaches the formulae of therapy; instead, she finds the best, most creative work comes from intuition and connection, when one is playing with feeling rather than merely playing the prescribed notes.

Of course, she admitted that without being drilled in the exercises, without practicing over and over again, she would not be able to draw on her vast experience from which to improvise. "I have a real understanding and appreciation of techniques but I am sure glad that I came through to the other side. I find it so much richer and much more rewarding. I am certain that my work is better because of it." This is not an either–or choice according to Weiner-Davis, but rather an ongoing process.

PLAYING BACK TAPES

Back to the illustrative case: The couple consisted of a special education teacher and a school administrator. "When she was speaking about her marriage during the session, it is almost like she had a chart with gold stars. She was very positive about recognizing small steps forward, almost too positive! Then you have her husband. He was a school administrator and he was kind of stiff. He always seemed critical. Every time his wife said something positive, he would respond by saying something negative. Because I was relatively new to the solution-focused stuff, I had it in my head that I was supposed to get these people to focus on positive things."

"What was different about your marriage when things were working?" Weiner-Davis asked the couple. Rather than responding as expected, the husband started talking about what wasn't working. Thinking that perhaps she had not been understood, she tried again.

"I hear that things aren't working, but there must have been a time in your marriage when things were better?" Weiner-Davis nodded to herself as she formed the question more clearly this time.

"Yeah," the husband admitted, "they weren't some of the things that I just mentioned but. . ." Then he launched into a whole other list of things that were not working in the marriage. Michele tried again a third time. Sure enough, the same thing happened.

"It is really powerful to see this on tape," Weiner-Davis explained. "My assessment at the time was that the husband refused to answer my question, refused to be positive. I diagnosed him instead of really understanding that this man had a story to tell, and that he didn't feel understood or heard. I continued along that path for another session or two." Then Michele relied on a technique she had often used with clients she deemed difficult.

"I thought the husband was being resistant so I applied one of my strategic techniques. I told them that I was really concerned about their marriage, that people with lesser problems were certainly able to pull themselves up by their bootstraps, but I was concerned about their ability to do that. I was doing this purely as a challenge because I felt they needed that.

"They came back a week later and you would not have recognized them. They were nothing at all like they had been. The husband was incredibly loving. He had done wonderful things for his wife. I was pretty proud of myself and my strategic intervention."

But now when Weiner-Davis plays the tape at workshops, she has a completely different take on things. She realizes that much of what she had said to him as part of her paradoxical directive were actually things the husband had been saying to her all along, things she had neither heard nor responded to.

"I finally realized that this man had felt ganged up on because his wife was so positive by nature and then I was so single-minded about focusing on all the positive stuff as well. I really missed the boat. For years I was showing this tape as an example of dealing with resistance in therapy and I finally figured out that *I* was the one being resistant."

MY WORST CRITIC

As Michele talked about how she screwed up, there was almost a giggle of amusement in her voice. This reminded us of the first thing she had said about how she was able to let go of things. One of the reasons why it was difficult for her to remember some of her mistakes was because she was really good at processing them and letting them go, learning from what happened and moving on. This was such an admirable gift, one that neither of us practices as much as we would like. We wondered if she'd be willing to talk more about how she does that. Each of us realized that when seeing clients in therapy, it was relatively easy to let go of bad work compared to when we were working in a more public forum. When doing workshops, teaching university classes, doing media interviews, or giving lectures to large audiences, almost every experience results in regrets about things we could have—or should have—done differently. "Why did I say that?" "Why didn't I do something else instead?" It might take 24 hours to let go of a bad therapy session but it seemed to take considerably longer to be forgiving about more public mistakes.

"I am also my worst critic in a lot of ways," Weiner-Davis agreed. "I can tell you that I can feel great about a workshop that I just did. I am higher than a kite but I will definitely think about things that I want to do differently next time."

"It's not like there haven't been failures in my career that haven't tripped me up, because there have. But I would say for the most part, I know in my heart that I am genuine in my efforts to help people and I am genuine about teaching other therapists. I know that I really do the best that I can. It's not always as good as I want it to be, but for the most part, I feel that I contribute something. Most of the time I choose to focus on what I bring to the experience rather than where I have failed."

Apparently, one of the important themes in Weiner-Davis' career has been helping people to focus on what is working well rather than dwelling on their problems. Another critical feature of her approach has been to practice what she preaches in her own life. As a "divorce buster," she takes great pride in maintaining a continually evolving love relationship with her life partner of three decades.

"I have a husband who is incredibly supportive of me and we process things a lot. He is a really big fan and cheerleader. During the times when I feel bad about something, he has been an amazing source of support. He moves me off dead center."

She went on to say, "I have always been fascinated with people who are truly successful in whatever line of work they do. They have enormous amounts of failures but what separates them from those who aren't as successful is a determination to not allow their failures to derail them very long. I like that."

Michele cited as an example of her own struggle not to allow herself to get derailed. She told us of a book she had written that she was sure was going to be a major bestseller. The book sold relatively poorly. "At that same time, I had a couple of other projects that fell through the cracks. This was the first time in my career that I had a major failure and then I had several smaller ones piled up on top of that. That took me a while to recover from." Michele stopped for a moment, wondering if she was off-track having drifted away from purely clinical cases. We encouraged her to continue as the principles were the same, so she related a particularly upsetting example that took place during a demonstration in front of a thousand people at professional conference.

A VERY PUBLIC FAILURE

"I was asked to do a demonstration and I told them that I would be really happy to do that but that I had several stipulations—I wanted to do marital therapy and show how I work with couples. Second, I was willing to work on any problem so long as it was a marital issue and that the demonstration couple was committed to staying together. Finally, I wanted my session to be an intake session. As it turned out, none of those things happened. The couple had been in therapy for a while and, just before they walked on stage, were coached to discuss an unexpected topic.

"There I was in front of a thousand people. When I asked the couple what they wanted to change about the marriage, the woman started to talk about the fact that she was afraid that her elder teenaged daughter was having an incestuous relationship with her younger sister.

"There was an audible gasp in the audience. That's how things got rolling. It just caught me so off guard, I could hardly think. I spent a long time afterwards wishing that it had never happened, wishing I had done things differently, wishing that I had ended the session abruptly saying that I would work with them privately; that this isn't a reasonable case for our demonstration.

"I remember coming home that night and saying to myself that I would never, ever do another presentation for as long as I live. Obviously, that didn't last too long. But that was a really, tough one for me."

We all agreed that the magnitude of perceived failure seemed proportionate to the size of the audience. When working alone with a single client, realizing our mistakes certainly stings a bit, especially if the person is somehow injured as a result of the miscalculation. But when the lapse occurs in front of a larger audience—a family, a group, a classroom, a conference presentation, a workshop, a national television audience, the residual shame is magnified many times.

We kidded Weiner-Davis about whether she ever goes back to that conference, or that when she goes, whether she disguises herself. We wondered how she let the mistake go, how she moved on afterwards. We were pressing her on this mostly because it is an area in which we both could use some more work ourselves. Also, since we've been talking to the world's best therapists for this project, what is the harm of seeking a little quick help for ourselves?

Weiner-Davis has attended that convention every year, but is quick to add that she still steers away from doing live demonstrations. This is a realization that several others mentioned as well, that the complex nature of doing work on stage, with the corresponding mixed agendas of all the participants, makes such public therapies unpredictable and sometimes even dangerous.

THERE'S ALWAYS NEXT TIME

Okay, we acknowledged, you decided not to repeat that mistake again. But how did you get over it? How did you let it go and move on?

"In regard to doing presentations, I had no choice to some extent. I had many commitments left to honor. I forced myself to get up there and do it. Feeling better about things though was another matter. It just took time. Actually, after mulling over criticisms about that demonstration I gave myself permission to recall many of the kind comments as well. I gradually decided that there had to be some truth to the positive feedback too. But it was hard. The criticisms hurt. What finally moved me forward was something a friend and colleague said to me. 'Michele, you know how successful you are by the size of the stones people throw at you.' I don't know how many years ago it was that I heard that, but it's not something I have ever forgotten."

What about some final words or best guidance to others about how to process their own failures and mistakes?

"They should use this philosophy: There is no such thing as failure, just useful feedback as to what to do next. I think it is pretty self-indulgent to sit around feeling really bad about yourself for mistakes that you have made rather than trying to figure out how you can do better the next time."

Chapter 23

SOME COMMON THEMES AND LESSONS LEARNED

We had been living with bad therapy for the better part of a year, listening to tales of woe, tragedy, and sometimes situation comedy. Our job had been essentially to get some very prominent and famous people, those who make a living from projecting an image of perfection, to admit and talk frankly about their miscues, mistakes, misjudgments, and miscalculations—in other words, to get them to talk openly, honestly, and publicly about their failures and imperfections.

In some ways, this was the ultimate job for a voyeur. Anyone who volunteered to be part of this project knew that we would be asking some very personal and intrusive questions about areas of their lives that have ordinarily been hidden from view. The question was not why any of the handful of people who declined the invitation chose not to participate but rather why the two dozen brave souls agreed to tell us their stories.

HOW FAILURE HELPS

Our participants seemed to agree that processing failures constructively is a big part of what makes them so good at what they do. They may not talk about their bad therapy that often in public forums, especially when people pay well-earned money to hear stories of miraculous success, but that is not to say that they don't reflect on these negative experiences quite a lot when they are in safe company.

It is clear from our interviews, as well as our own research, that acknowledging and working through our failures can help in a number of ways:

- *Promoting reflective activity.* A number of contributors remarked about how many years, even decades, they had been processing their mistakes. Even those who are good at forgiving their lapses, letting go of their mistakes, still invest a lot of time and energy figuring out what went wrong and what they might do differently next time. In fact, perhaps one of the distinguishing characteristics of this august group is that they were intensely interested in working as hard as they could to get better and better at what they do. This could only come from identifying their weaknesses and building on what they do best.

- *Providing useful information.* One way of looking at ineffective therapeutic efforts is that they represent mere feedback along the path toward eventual success. So many of the master therapists mentioned the importance of the therapeutic relationship in their work because, with sufficient trust developed, clients will be patient enough until we find the right combination of methods that make the most difference. Failure is not even part of the vocabulary of some professionals, as they see this as only an interim judgment about progress but not necessarily the final result.

- *Fostering flexibility.* Anyone can follow a formula or structured methodology. What led the experts to continued development in their work was the recognition that what they were doing was not working and then being prepared to abandon that strategy in favor of others within their repertoire. A general principle seemed to emerge in our discussions in which the more flexible a clinician could be, the more likely that bad therapy could be avoided. Of course, this all hangs on the assumption that the practitioner has a general plan, an idea of how therapy works, and the best ways to help people.

- *Requiring patience.* Therapy ends unsuccessfully at the point at which one or both participants give up. So long as the partners in the process are willing to be patient with one another, maintain realistic expectations about what is possible, and forgive one another for miscalculations, eventually some satisfactory solution will almost always emerge.

- *Teaching humility.* Several of the contributors mentioned that in bad therapy, narcissism got in the way. The therapist's need to be right, to win power struggles, to repeatedly "prove" the correctness of a theory, can be a huge impediment to listening more carefully to clients, and responding to their needs. Facing our mistakes and failures teaches us to be more accepting of our limits and more willing to acknowledge that we aren't nearly as important as we'd like to be.

WHAT WE LEARNED FROM THIS EXPERIENCE

In addition to the consensus that there is value in acknowledging our lousy work more honestly and openly, we learned several other things from this study. In this closing chapter, we would like to review some of the themes, lessons, and principles that stand out most.

What Struck Us Most

It was humbling to listen to such bright, experienced, articulate people talk about their work. Both of us are pretty good talkers but we were still amazed at the high level of verbal fluency of these professionals. They spoke with such clarity, making complex ideas so understandable. It was not just what they had to say that was so interesting but it was also the power of their voices.

If you have ever wondered why certain members of our profession receive such notoriety and attention because of their written work, let us tell you that they are also very good talkers. Essentially, we were asking people to talk about the most difficult parts of what they do for a living, and we were amazed at how clearly and poetically they expressed themselves.

Second, we noticed that many of the contributors found it much easier to talk about failures that occurred a long time in the past rather than those closer to the present. Failure was viewed by most as an historical phenomenon rather than a current struggle. Our contributors were willing to participate in the study, but some were not willing to go as deep, or as far, as we had hoped.

We suspect that one reason for this is because it was a lot more comfortable to discuss a phenomenon that had already been thoroughly worked through rather than one that was still raw, confusing, and fresh. As one would expect, there was also a lot of caution related to image management. These are people who make a living based on their reputations so there would, understandably, be some reluctance to portray oneself in less than a favorable light.

We were both delighted and amazed by how much all of our contributors still enjoy doing therapy and love what they are doing. This may have been more surprising to Jeffrey than Jon, since he had become burned out after full-time practice for many years and was only just now slowly beginning to see clients again.

We were also struck by how difficult it was for several of the participants to think of examples of bad therapy. Even with many weeks advance notice, some of the contributors could barely think of a single instance in which they had clearly failed their clients. This was so different from our own experience in which not a single week goes by that we can't point to some bungled effort that we wish we could have done differently.

What Surprised Us

It was interesting to hear people talk in ways that seemed a far cry from their espoused theories. Many who were known primarily for their rather structured therapies and specific techniques talked like raging humanists in their concern for relationships and the value of caring. We noticed that many of these theorists had moved way beyond their early work (that is still being practiced as originally conceived) and embraced a more global, universal practice that borrowed ideas from one another.

It was surprising how many of the participants needed structure for the conversation and were reluctant to go beyond the scheduled outline. There was a marked lack of spontaneity in many of the conversations which made our jobs more difficult in eliciting something new and interesting that hadn't been said before. Of course, it makes perfect sense to be cautious and careful in such risky enterprise in which we were asking such personal questions.

We were surprised, but not surprised, that several of the participants needed, or wanted, reassurance about how they were doing. They wanted to know how they stood compared to others. We would have felt (and do) exactly the same way, which is why this should not have surprised us.

Some Common Themes

There was a universal belief among the contributors that talking about bad therapy was a very good idea. Processing mistakes and failures had greatly shaped their ideas and practice. Their bad therapy was seminal for them in terms of refining their strategies and improving their effectiveness. Most of the contributors were quite skilled at letting go of their lousy work. They were forgiving of their mistakes; they viewed them as the inevitable result of doing their jobs.

We discovered an interesting parallel between our own styles and those of the people we interviewed. While Jon doesn't dwell on failures, Jeffrey spends a lot of time thinking about what he could have done differently. In a similar vein, most of the professionals we spoke to could be grouped according to this typology: the "dwellers" or the "shruggers." The latter group of practitioners just expects to screw up on occasion, so when this inevitably occurs, they are not unduly bothered by the experience.

Similarities and Differences in the Stories

The biggest similarity is the convergence of ideas going on in the field in which everyone is using everyone else's ideas. Approaches that were known for rather specific complaints have now become universalized to a broad range of problems. Almost everyone talked, in some capacity, about how important relationships are with their clients, how they get in trouble when they fall in love with techniques.

Perhaps the greatest difference between them was the language they used. Oftentimes, four or five different people would talk about essentially the same idea, but use language suited to their conceptual frameworks. No wonder it is sometimes hard for us to talk to one another.

Another thing the contributors shared was a strong ambition for recognition, a drive that we readily own. Many of these high-achieving folks are at the pinnacle of their careers, at a point where they have created a legacy that they now wish to protect. That is one reason why what we asked them to do—talk about their fallibility and imperfections—was so challenging. That is also one reason why the cases they selected to talk about were those they could readily explain, or at times, write off as the result of factors outside of their control.

This got us thinking about how rare it is that we ever hear another professional admit: (1) I blew it; (2) It is all my fault; (3) I didn't see it coming; and (4) I don't know why it happened. Instead, we are inclined to make up excuses, identify scapegoats and extenuating circumstances, create elaborate explanations for what happened and why, and convince ourselves (and others) that we can somehow prevent such lapses in the future.

What We Learned About Therapy

There is still so much we don't know and don't understand about what we do. After listening to each of the master practitioners talk about what they do, and how they do it, we were struck by the incredible expertise that people have that is beyond our own experience. Yet for Jon, the conversations were very affirming in realizing that he can hold his own with anyone else. He has never felt better about the way he works with clients and the results that he gets. Jon has had the opportunity to work closely with many of these great therapists and he thinks that a lot of their magic must have rubbed off on him.

What Jeffrey Learned About Jon

I (Jeffrey) learned just how much I trust Jon, how great it feels to work with a partner where we can practically read one another's minds. I was in awe of Jon's ability to listen carefully. And I am greatly envious of the ways he gives people the benefit of the doubt. Granted, most of the contributors were personal friends, but at times when I was feeling critical or frustrated, Jon almost always responded in a compassionate and understanding way. As a result of this collaboration, I have resolved to work more on following what Jon has modeled for me in this dimension.

I also learned about differences in the ways we manage our lives. So much of Jon's life is partitioned into 30-minute segments that it might take weeks for us to coordinate our schedules, before we could schedule a conversation. I wonder why Jon works so hard, why he juggles so many things, why his life is so busy. Most of all, this has helped me to *unstructure* my life more, to save more space for play. This has occurred, in part, by having such an intimate window into another's world, especially someone I so greatly admire and respect.

What Jon Learned About Jeffrey

I (Jon) appreciate Jeffrey's insight. He has great compassion and caring for others. Yet I like the way he pushes people. He keeps wanting to go further, to push people to look at themselves more deeply. This is what he does. He take things to a personal level.

I learned that Jeffrey really wants to be seen as someone who is helpful. This is important to him, and who he is. Yet he seems more worried about this than he needs to be.

I learned that Jeffrey is very playful and a lot of fun. He is unpredictable at times, much more so than others I've been around. I like that, his creativity and spontaneity. He has boundless energy and so many interests. He likes to push the edges of what he can do.

I also learned what a clever writer Jeffrey is. He is a magician with words. Although the content of each chapter came from the expert, Jeffrey made the material come alive.

What We Learned About Ourselves

After hearing so many great therapists talk about their work, and hearing the continual joy and satisfaction they derive from seeing clients, I (Jeffrey) resolved to get more into active practice. Because of my travel schedule, I had stopped seeing regular clients for a while but now I intend to start up again. In fact, I can't wait to get started.

I learned that there are things I don't know nearly as well as others whom I admire—mostly I want to listen better and respond more compassionately. But I also learned that there are things that I do better than most. I realized how flexible I am, how open I am to new learning. I also confronted how defensive I feel when my most sacred ideas are challenged (or ridiculed) by others who hold a different ideology. I guess I knew that already, but I have never felt this stuff more closely in my face.

I (Jon) learned to be even more forgiving of my bad therapy and mistakes. I have found more courage to fail, and feel okay about that. I also realize how busy I am on so many levels. I try to stay focused and task oriented. I juggle a lot of things at the same time. This makes me very productive. But I impose my pace on others. For some people, this works well, but for others it doesn't fit at all. I realize that is a major source of my bad therapy, yet I am still puzzled why others don't push themselves harder.

What Was Most Difficult For Jeffrey

It is easier for me to talk about the professional stuff before the personal. It was certainly challenging to get our participants to go deeper than they wanted to go. Their jobs were often to hide as much as they could and our jobs were to bring them out as much as they were willing: this was sometimes frustrating because the results were less than I wanted. But then again, getting rid of expectations is still one of my lifelong issues.

To move on to the personal, one of the main issues that emerged for me was the strong desire to be "seen" and "heard" by others whom I admire. This is about my lifelong struggle for recognition and validation that has led me to become such a devoted student of failure, and pushed me to be so overly productive.

I was surprised, first of all, by how little many of the contributors wanted to engage me on any level. I can think of only two or three instances in which people even used my name. At first, I felt invisible, or at the very least, irrelevant. I tried extra hard during the subsequent interviews to provoke the participants in some way so, at the very least, they would know that I was there. But I still didn't feel very often that I was acknowledged explicitly by many of the people we talked to about such intimate subjects.

One reason for the lack of engagement was the structure we introduced that was time-limited and very much connected to managing time. I know that, in part, another reason for this is because most of the contributors were friends and long-time associates of Jon. The reason these folks agreed to participate in such a risky endeavor was because of the trusting relationships they enjoyed with him. But I was still struck (and a bit hurt) that very few people had any apparent interest in knowing who I am.

Now, I suspect that much of this perception is based on my own stuff, which is why I've included these remarks in this section on what I've learned about myself and what I've found most difficult to admit. I don't like the part of me that feels competitive, that wants to know where I stand in relation to the best in my field. I wish I cared a whole lot less about what anyone thought of me. But I *do* care. Intensely.

A related issue that I learned about myself has to do with the "ownership" of ideas. I know I share this struggle with most of the contributors because a big theme already mentioned was how important their legacies were. Some contributors spent considerable time promoting their ideas rather than focusing on the topic of bad therapy; it was as if their life mission was to spread the word of truth as they know it—and to be acknowledged publicly for their contributions.

It has been over 20 years since I've written about failure and it was interesting to hear others talk about things I've said as if they were their own ideas. Now perhaps they are and were developed independently, but that is not the point of my insight: it is that I care, that I want credit. Again that theme pops up about wanting to be seen and heard.

I also was confronted with a lot more work I have to do related to letting go of my bad therapy (and mistakes in all areas of my life). I noticed that several (if not most) of the contributors were quite skilled at forgiving themselves for their failures, letting them go, and moving on. Yet I tend to dwell on them, relive them over and over again, berate myself for not getting things right.

Right now, I am in a new administrative position at a new institution in a new part of the country. As I would expect in such a situation, I am confused much of the time and have little idea what I'm doing. In the span of a few weeks, I've had to learn a new culture, new institutional procedures, new policies and norms, hundreds of new people, and a new job that has been vacant for so many years that it will take a long time to sort things out. While I relish and enjoy the challenges (and enjoy the work), I make dozens of mistakes every day. I give bad advice to students (this is easy to do because I can't even remember which course numbers belong to which names). I am supposed to be mentoring other faculty but, because I'm untenured myself, I am not allowed access to their files. Well, you get the point.

I recently wrote an e-mail to a friend, giving her an update on how things were going (mostly well), how I feel about the people I work with (mostly great), and some challenges I'm facing (quite a long list). But when it came time to send the message off, I inadvertently added the wrong address—the one that goes to *all* the faculty in my department. Now, as it turns out, there was nothing in the message that I wouldn't have said to any of them anyway. And second, it was an understandable error for someone new to the system, someone who had never used a PC before after a lifetime of devotion to Macintosh computers. This didn't mean I was stupid (I told myself over and over again). This didn't mean I was incompetent (I repeated like a mantra). Yet it has been months since this incident and I still rehash it and berate myself in my head.

Am I proud of this? Heck no. Should I get back into therapy to work on this stuff? Probably so. I mention this theme, and this illustrative example, just to demonstrate how I have been impacted most by this project. Listening to this group of master therapists, hearing how they process their own mistakes, has led me to conclude that it is time, once and for all, that I learn to accept my imperfections. Of course, if I do that, I'll have to find something else to write about in the future (that's just my resistance and denial kicking in).

One result of this project for me is that I ended up getting vicarious, indirect therapy from 20 of the best practitioners in the world. I couldn't help but personalize much of what we were talking about, continually asking myself what this had to do with my own life. Since the subject of failure is the single recurrent issue in my life, this whole project has been an exercise in personal and professional growth for me. It will take me many years to process all that I've learned.

What Was Most Difficult For Jon

I didn't find this project that difficult; it was a pleasure, a welcome diversion from all the other things I do in my life. I found the people really easy to work with and as cooperative as I expected.

I guess one thing that bothered me was feeling the struggle and the pain of the contributors. At times, I wanted to reach out and help them. I kept biting my tongue. I wanted to respond to them as a therapist rather than as an interviewer.

I was a bit disappointed that our questions did not help some of the contributors go deeper. At times, I felt disappointed that we didn't go deeper than we did.

So, What Is Bad Therapy Anyway?

There were several distinct ways that bad therapy, or clinical failure, was defined by our esteemed contributors. While you will notice themes and elements in common, there are also almost a dozen distinct facets that were identified.

- When the therapist does not listen to the client and instead follows his or her own agenda (Arnold Lazarus, Violet Oaklander).
- Making the same mistakes over and over again (Jon Carlson, Michele Weiner-Davis).
- Inflexibility and reluctance to make needed adjustments (Ray Corsini, John Norcross, Peggy Papp, Dick Stuart).

- Not knowing where you are going (Art Freeman).
- Arrogance, overconfidence, therapist's narcissism (Art Freeman, Bill Glasser, Arnie Lazarus).
- An internal feeling of ineptitude (Sam Gladding, Jeffrey Kottler, Michael Hoyt, Peggy Papp).
- Failure to create a solid alliance (Bill Glasser, Arnie Lazarus, Sue Johnson, Jeffrey Kottler).
- Using obsolete methods (Len Sperry, John Gray).
- Negative outcomes for the client (Michael Hoyt, Steve Lankton, Scott Miller, Dick Stuart).
- Losing control of self or countertransference issues (Pat Love, John Norcross, Dick Schwartz, Len Sperry).
- Making invalid assumptions (Frank Pittman, Francine Shapiro).

Many of the contributors would agree that the rest of the items on the list are also strong indicators of bad therapy, but based on what they revealed in their discussions, these are the features they considered most important.

In summary, bad therapy occurs when either the client or the therapist is not satisfied with the result, and when that outcome can be traced to the therapist's repeated miscalculations, misjudgments, or mistakes.

In one sense, all therapy is bad therapy since we can never meet our own unrealistic expectations for perfection. We can rarely, if ever, exert the kind of influence that we would prefer. We can never cure all the suffering we see. We cannot possibly execute our techniques, practice our clinical skills, or implement our strategies in the flawless, effortless way that we plan things in our head. We are doomed to fail, destined to be imperfect. If bad therapy is when one or both of us is unsatisfied, then all therapy is indeed short of the mark.

Yet on the other hand (you knew this was coming), no matter what we do, and how we do it, clients often get some benefit from the encounter, often something very different from what we had intended—or what they expected. In that sense, all therapy can be good therapy, depending on how it was received.

We have learned that confessing mistakes often deepens relationships. You'll have to consider that yourself when you reassess your personal reactions to us, and to the various contributors to this project. Do you now look at us with increasing skepticism and with less respect? Or, as we suspect, did our confessions help you to like and trust us more? That is the curious thing about talking about our imperfections in an open and honest way. We need to develop more courage to speak more openly about our failures.

Where Do You Go From Here?

If we have been successful in our efforts, then you may be feeling more willing to talk about your mistakes and failures to others, to learn from these experiences in more constructive ways instead of living with them in secrecy and shame, instead of hiding them in coded notes or recurrent nightmares of discovery.

We hope that you have found that therapy, like life in general, involves continual failure and correction. No matter how good you are as a practitioner, even if you are considered one of the "notable figures" in the field, your next bad therapy is just around the corner.

REFERENCES

Bugental, J. F. T. (1988). What is failure in psychotherapy? *Psychotherapy, 25,* 532–535.

Coleman, S. B. (Ed.). (1985). *Failures in family therapy.* New York: Guilford.

Conyne, R. K. (1999). *Failures in group work.* Thousand Oaks, CA: Sage.

Estrada, A. U., & Homes, J. M. (1999). Couples' perception of effective and ineffective ingredients in marital therapy. *Journal of Sex and Marital Therapy, 25,* 151–162.

Hill, C. E., Nutt-Williams, E., Heaton, K. J., Thompson, B. J., & Rhodes, R. H. (1996). Therapist retrospective recall of impasses in long-term psychotherapy: A qualitative analysis. *Journal of Counseling Psychology, 43,* 207–217.

Hollon, S. D. (1995). Failure in psychotherapy. *Journal of Psychotherapy Integration, 5*(2), 171–175.

Keith, D. V., & Whitaker, C. A. (1985). Failure: Our bold companion. In S. B. Coleman (Ed.), *Failures in family therapy* (pp. 8–23). New York: Guilford.

Kottler, J. A. (2001). *Making changes last.* New York: Brunner/Routledge.

Kottler, J. A., & Blau, D. S. (1989). *The imperfect therapist: Learning from failure in therapeutic practice.* San Francisco: Jossey-Bass.

Papp, P. (1985). Foreword. In S. B. Coleman (Ed.), *Failures in family therapy.* New York: Guilford.

Robertiello, R. C., & Schoenewolf, G. (1987). *101 common therapeutic blunders: Countertransference and counterresistance in psychotherapy.* Northvale, NJ: Jason Aronson.

Stiles, W. B., Gordon, L. E., & Lani, J. A. (2002). Session evaluation and the session evaluation questionnaire. In G. S. Tryon (Ed.), *Counseling based on process research: Applying what we know* (pp. 325–343). Boston: Allyn and Bacon.